THE LAST OF THE SWEET BANANAS

JACK MAPANJE

THE LAST OF THE
SWEET BANANAS
◆ NEW & SELECTED POEMS ◆

BLOODAXE BOOKS

in association with
THE WORDSWORTH TRUST

ISBN: 1 85224 665 0

First published 2004 by
Bloodaxe Books Ltd,
Highgreen,
Tarset,
Northumberland NE48 1RP,
in association with
The Wordsworth Trust,
Dove Cottage, Grasmere,
Cumbria LA22 9SH.

Second impression 2005.

www.bloodaxebooks.com
For further information about Bloodaxe titles
please visit our website or write to
the above address for a catalogue.

Bloodaxe Books Ltd acknowledges
the financial assistance of
Arts Council England, North East.

Cover printing by J. Thomson Colour Printers Ltd, Glasgow.

Printed in Great Britain by
Cromwell Press Ltd, Trowbridge, Wiltshire.

For Mercy Angela, Judith Dalitso,
Lunda Pilira, Likambale David.

Acknowledgements

This book draws on Jack Mapanje's four previous collections: *Mau* (Hetherwick Press, Malawi, 1971), *Of Chameleons and Gods* (Heinemann Educational Books, 1981), *The Chattering Wagtails of Mikuyu Prison* (Heinemann Educational Books, 1993), *Skipping Without Ropes* (Bloodaxe Books, 1998).

Other poems have previously been appeared in *The Shop* (Republic of Ireland, 1999), *Stand Magazine* (1999), and *A Winter Garland* (The Wordsworth Trust, 2004); and some were broadcast by BBC Radio 4 (2003).

CONTENTS

From *The Chattering Wagtails Of Mikuyu Prison* (1993)

ix

New Poems

INTRODUCTION

I WAS BORN under British colonial rule and matured under the Republic of Malawi. Specifically, I grew up and started school before the British Protectorate of Nyasaland was forced into the Central African Federation of Southern Rhodesia (Zimbabwe), Northern Rhodesia (Zambia) and Nyasaland (Malawi). I went to universities in Malawi and London after Nyasaland had broken away from the Central African Federation and gained independence under Dr Hastings Kamuzu Banda. Perhaps it is because Nyasaland was the most economically, socially and culturally disadvantaged of the Federation Triangle (though the richest in human resources) that my life has tended to be a constant struggle against the despotic structures that keep ordinary people silent and make them invisible. I have in mind those strictures that manifested themselves officially as the Special Powers Acts, Emergency Provisions Acts, Prevention of Terrorism Acts, Censorship Acts and others, which were established by British colonial rule and exploited to the full by the Central African Federation and Hastings Banda's thirty years of totalitarian rule.

Throughout my career as an academic and writer I have been fascinated by the resilience that the small people of the world (the old, the young, the women and those that are considered minorities) develop against the global interventions of the powerful. My narrative verse has often asserted the identity and integrity of the people on the periphery and implicitly called for the restitution of their dignity. Sometimes I have found myself shamelessly becoming the self-appointed spokesperson for the so-called 'dregs of society'. I know I am not qualified for the post, but through my verse, I just find myself defending those who seem unable to defend themselves, intrinsically suggesting creative strategies against political, social and cultural structures that imprison the human spirit and erase creative endeavour and energy. Naturally, I consider the division often made between politics and poetry to be thin and contrived, for, throughout my life politics and poetry have been so intricately intertwined that they seem inseparable.

This is perhaps understandable given the historical background I grew up under. As soon as Banda assumed the political and administrative control of Malawi from the British, he created a cabinet crisis which permanently split his government, the country and our psyches. In defence of their position Banda and his hench persons established what became one of independent Africa's most autocratic regime. His political party machinery, ran by brutal Young Pioneers and the Youth League, was so authoritarian that it disrupted people's daily activities, movements and lives. Banda blatantly placed the Young Pioneers and the Youth Leaguers above law – the police did not dare to bring them to book for the crimes they committed against the people. He created traditional courts which pretty much rubberstamped his decisions and the desires of his 'inner circle' on matters that concerned politics, including such matters as to who was considered 'rebel' and who was not; who was to be deported, eliminated, imprisoned and who merely encouraged into exile.

The censorship board, which was created specially to vet and police the films we watched, the books, magazines and newspapers we read, and the internal and external radio programmes we listened to, is still remembered for its notoriety today. Almost everything political, social and cultural was stringently controlled; beliefs and views that questioned authority or exposed hypocrisy or suggested democratic approaches to national problems, however constructively, were unacceptable, whether they were internally or externally generated. Engaging in serious activity such as academic research, producing plays, writing poetry or short stories, painting or sculpting was, therefore, a hazardous business. One had to be given 'official clearance' for every research project, manuscript of a play, poem or story – every item of cultural interest – before embarking on the project, production, publication or viewing. Banda and his coterie adopted an arrogant stance which encouraged most creative people to work surreptitiously. They openly claimed that only they knew and understood what was best for the development of the country – our views on matters that concerned our nation were irrelevant to them. Dissenting politicians, religious leaders, academics, lawyers, journalists, writers and ordinary urban or rural people were indiscriminately arrested, imprisoned or encouraged into exile, often without charge or trial. Thousands of innocent people were 'accidentalised' during Banda's thirty years of despotic rule; thousands upon thousands of 'prisoners of conscience' died in Malawi's prisons; some languished in prisons for periods of up to twentyeight years, without trial, charge or proper explanation.

I myself was lucky to have been imprisoned for only three years seven months sixteen days and more than twelve hours at the notorious Mikuyu Prison. But neither at my arrest and detention nor at my release was I told what crime I had committed – you did not need to commit a crime to be arrested, imprisoned or encouraged into exile. Apparently it was the many conflicting interpretations of the poems in my book, *Of Chameleons and Gods,* most of them included in this volume, and the negative implications drawn by Banda's and his coterie's informers from the short introduction I provided to the book, which caused the furore that led to my detention. This is what I said:

> The verse in this volume spans some ten turbulent years in
> which I have been attempting to find a voice or voices as a way
> of preserving some sanity. Obviously where personal voices are
> too easily muffled, this is a difficult task; one is tempted like
> the chameleon, who failed to deliver Chiuta's message of life,
> to bask in one's brilliant camouflage. But the exercise has been,
> if nothing else, therapeutic; and that's no mean word in our
> circumstances.

Yet the supposition that it was these words which so angered Banda's 'inner circle' that they recommended my incarceration is speculative, as I was not even taken to their 'traditional courts', if only to be falsely accused of treason!

It is for this reason that I did not bother to write introductions to the two books of poems that followed: *The Chattering Wagtails of Mikuyu Prison* and *Skipping Without Ropes,* whose verse constitutes the bulk of this selection. Now that the political landscape of Malawi has somewhat changed, the context for the cryptic verse we once wrote can be provided without fear – hence the slight changes to titles of some poems and the addition of dedications, footnotes and dates to others. The new poems in the final section of this volume are free from cryptic language. *The Last of the Sweet Bananas* represents the most substantive body of my poetry to date that I would like to share with my family, relatives, friends, compatriots, acquaintances, special strangers and lovers of poetry in general. The title is taken from the last line of the poem 'When The Shire Valley Dries Up Patiently'.

Finally, I would like to thank Neil Astley, Editor of Bloodaxe Books, and Robert Woof, Director of the Wordsworth Trust, for their encouragement, and for jointly publishing this collection, and so making available once again poems that were originally published by the now discontinued Heinemann African Writers Series. My debt to Stephen Hebron, who has set the text, is immense.

Grasmere, 2004

From
Mau (1971) and
Of Chameleons And Gods (1981)

The New Platform Dances

Haven't I danced the big dance,
Compelled the rains so dust could
Soar high above like when animals
Stampede? Haven't I in animal
Skins wriggled with amulets
Rattled with anklets
Scattered nervous women
With snakes around my neck
With spears in these hands
Then enticed them back
With fly whisk's magic?
Haven't I moved with all
Concentric in the arena
To the mystic drums
Dancing the half-nude
Lomwe dance
Haven't I?

Haven't my wives at mortars sang
Me songs of praise, of glory,
How I quaked the earth
How my skin trembled
How my neck peaked
Above all dancers
How my voice throbbed
Like the father-drum
I danced to
Haven't they?

Now, when I see my daughters writhe
Under cheating abstract
Voices of slack drums, ululate
To babble-idea-men-masks

Without amulets and anklets,
Why don't I stand up
To show them how we danced
Chopa, how IT was born?
Why do I sit still
Why does my speech choke
Like I have not danced
Before? Haven't I
Danced the bigger dance?
Haven't I?

When This Carnival Finally Closes

When this frothful carnival finally closes, brother,
When your drumming veins dry, these very officers
Will burn the scripts of the praises we sang to you
And shatter the calabashes you drank from. Your
Charms, these drums, and the effigies blazing will
Become the accomplices to your lie-achieved world!
Your bamboo hut on the beach, they'll make a bonfire
Under the cover of giving their hero a true traditional
Burial, though in truth to rid themselves of another
Deadly spirit that might otherwise have haunted them,
And at the wake new mask dancers will quickly leap
Into the arena dancing to tighter skins, boasting
Other clans of calabashes as the undertakers jest:
What did he think he would become, a God? The devil!

Making Our Clowns Martyrs

We all know why you have come back home with no
National colours flanking your black Mercedes Benz;
The radio said the toilets in the banquet halls of your
Dream have grown green creepers and cockroaches
Which won't flush; and the orders you once shouted
To the concubines so mute have now locked you in;
Hard luck my friend. But we all know what currents
Have stroked your temper. You come from a breed of
Toxic frogs croaking beside the smoking marshes of
River Shire, and the first words you breathed were
Snapped by the lethal mosquitoes of that morass. We
Knew you would wade your way through the arena
Though we wondered how you'd got chosen for the Benz.
You should have been born up the hills, brother, where
Lake waters swirl and tempers deepen with each season
Of the rains; there you'd have seen how the leopards of
Dedza hills comb the land or hedge before their assault.
But welcome back to the broken reed-fences, brother,
Welcome home to the poached reed-huts you left behind,
Welcome to these stunted pit-latrines where only
The pungent whiff of buzzing green flies gives way.
You will find your idle ducks still shuffle and fart
In large amounts; the black dog you left still sniffs
Distant recognition, lying, licking its leg wounds. And
Should the relatives greet you with nervous curiosity
In the manner of masks carved in somebody's image,
There's always across the dusty road your mad auntie;
She alone still thinks this new world is going shit; she
Alone still cracks about why where 'whys' are crimes.

Messages

1

Tell her we still expose our bottoms
Eat unseasoned *nsima* with *bonongwe**
From a wooden ladle, our hands unscented,
We still sleep in slums rolling
In bird-droppings, friends of fleas,
Maggots. Tell her our pleasure
Is still in the pattering tin-drums
That convoke these tatters in the cold
Of dawn to quench hangovers. Tell
Her besides, a cat sees best at night
Not much at noon and so when time
Comes, while she eats and drinks
While she twists and shouts, rides
And travels, we shall refuse
To reach her our stuff of fortune
Even if she called us witches!
We swear by our fathers dead!

3

Did you think it was a hunting party
Where after a fall from chasing a hare
You laughed together, an enemy shaking
Dust off your bottom, a friend reaching
You your bow and arrow? Or a game safari
Where you patted your hounds before
The halloo? Did you think this the bush
Where the party would take the best of
Their kill to the Chief so he could allow
Them more hunting bush next time? No,
Mother, it's a war here, a lonely war

Where you hack your own way single-handed
To make anything up to the Shaka of
The tribe! It's fine the earth is fertile!

Maize meal; unsavoury vegetables

Steve Biko Is Dead

The Boers have poked another
Human's sparkling eyes
With electronic tongs
Soldering his sharp brain to metal

Steve Biko is dead
The most liberal of Western
Papers will probably
Report his death thus:

'The duffers have wafted
Biko with another poisonous wand
Of a gorgeous apartheid peacock
Ogling sanity into slumber ...'

That Steve Biko was another Man
With a wife, a child, a conscience
And the right to live ordinarily
Fighting in peace,

Of the restive ship behind,
Why or for how long
Steve Bikos will waste,
We'll not bother to ask.

Who dares to budge
These precious days
And give evidence
For hope bereft?

After Wiriyamu Village
Massacre By Portuguese

No, go back into your exile, go back quick.
When those Portuguese soldiers abducted
Falencha's baby quietly strapped on her back
And scattered its precious brain on Falencha's
Own maize grinding stone, when those soldiers
Grabbed and hacked Dinyero's only son
With Dinyero herself stubbornly watching
Or when they burnt down Faranando in his own
Hut as he tried to save Alefa his senile wife –
Where, where was your hand? Tell me that!
And if you helped Fr Adrian Hastings report
The Portuguese atrocities to humans, where,
Where is your verse? You have no shame!
No, go back until our anger has simmered.

Messages From Soweto

'Go back to develop your own homelands!'

Today, they have set up mirrors
that reflect their ageing arrogance,
adopting a stern detrimental line –
They alone know what to think.

In the dark rooms of our universe
negatives assume the power of their original
images, naïve termites are unleashed –
To diet on the meagre corner-poles of our globe.

Exampli gratia, the other week:
colourful tadpoles hop about
the fringes of our dim pavements –
In the sometimes cool rains –

Didn't they become subversive
metaphors confusing the Michelin tyres
that crushed them! Even to pee –
Which youth does not need clearance?

Kabula Curio-Shop, Blantyre

Black wood between carefully bowed legs
The eyes red over bellows and smoke
The sharpening of axes, adzes, carvers
The chopping, the whittling and such
Carving such scooping and scooping
Then the sand-papering and smoothing

Black wood between carefully bowed legs
Such energy release and the price
Bargained away, would you imagine
Now a broken symbol thrown careless
In the nook of a curio-shop: a lioness
Broken legs, broken neck, broken udder?

The Cheerful Girls At Smiller's Bar, 1971

The prostitutes at Smiller's Bar beside the dusty road
Were only girls once, in tremulous mini-skirts and oriental
Beads, cheerfully swigging Carlsbergs and bouncing to
Rusty *simanje-manje* and *rumba* booming in the juke-box;
They were striking virgins bored by our Presbyterian
Prudes until a true Presbyterian came one night. And like
To us all, the girls offered him a seat on cheap planks
In the dark backyard room choked with diesel-oil clouds
From a tin-can lamp. Touched the official rolled his eyes
To one in style. She said no; most girls only wanted
A husband to hook or the fruits of independence to taste;
But since then mini-skirts were banned and the girls
Of Smiller's Bar were 'ugly prostitutes to boot!'

Today, the girls still giggle about what came through
The megaphones: the preservation of our traditional
et cetera, et cetera, et cetera ...

Cycles

1. Requiem To A Fallen Son

I still remember the songs,
The happy songs by the chaperons
Of our village in the middle of the night –
The child is born gods bless him
The child is here spirits spare him
The child is male witches protect him –
The ululations confirmed
A sure-footed birth
As the village blazed in bonfires
Dustbin drums carelessly talking.
'How the mother giggled digging up
The child from an anthill!'
Mother told us at the fireside.
And if there was blood
In the breaking of the cord
They must have made sure to hide it
For I saw, I felt, I smelt nothing
But the happiness of men and women
Reeling to taut drums
Roaring in jubilation of your birth, Son.

2. An Elegy For Mangochi Fishermen

Today the fireflies have become
The banners of our night fishermen
The crabs and *dondolos* dare not
Peep out of their crevices;

The virgin canoe we once boasted about
Holding the head or pushing the rear

Pulling the lips or rolling on poles,
The canoe has capsized, the carvers

Drowned. Those loin-cloths dripping,
The muscles twitching with power,
The husky voices chanting about
The delicious chambo dishes

Expected, even the toes once crushed
Dragging our canoe from the arid
Namizimu mountains to the soft
Beaches of this golden lake –

We will not cast in tender herbs to cure.
Today, you gone, the vigil wax has melted away,
The light is out in our cryptic recesses,
We must all lie in pitch dark stakes.

Should we then wipe our sticky brows
In the heat of another October? Should we fell
More poles to roll another canoe to the beach?
Is it worth it assembling another voice?

3. Before Chilembwe* Tree

I

Didn't you say we should trace
Your footsteps unmindful of
Quagmires, thickets and rivers
Until we reached your *nsolo* tree?

Now, here I seat my gourd of beer,
On my little fire, throw my millet
Flour and my smoked meat while
I await the second coming

II

Why does your mind boggle –
Who will offer another gourd
Who will force another step
To hide our shame?

The goat blood on the rocks
The smoke that issued
The drums you danced to
And the rains hoped for –

You've chanted yourselves hoarse,
Chilembwe is gone up in your dust;
Stop lingering then:
Who will start another fire?

*John Chilembwe was the first nationalist to fight for freedom
and independence from British rule in Nyasaland (Malawi) in
what eminent historian George Shepperson called 'The Chilembwe
Uprising'.

4. The Palm Trees At Chigawe

You stood like women in green
Proud travellers in panama hats and java print
Your fruit milk caused monkeys and shepherds to scramble
Your dry leaves were banners for night fishermen
But now stunted trees stand still beheaded –
A curious sight for the tourists.

5. *A Marching Litany To Our Martyrs*

In the name of our dear brothers dead
Are we really marching to these tin-drums
Rattling the skeleton beat of heroic
Bones long laid to sleep?

The planes that dropped white emergency papers

Do we really halt to revere perplexed
Elders now only shades shaking and
Tossing synthetic calabashes of *chibuku*
Beer which numbs their brain?

The stooges' cars and houses fire-gutted

Have we really about swung
To frantic maxi-skirts slit to thighs
Opening to whispers and caresses of
Midnight breezes and coins?

The barricades and bridges shattered

Do we now salute the squealing laughters
Of the broken hearts in their shells
Clicking their crumpled tin-cans of
Goat-urine to their bungled dreams?

What of the tear-gas and bullets on their heads?

Do we now troop past the skeletal mothers
Before their sons' burial mounds weeping
With broken bowls of rotten weevils
And shards of sour brew for their libation?

And those bitter tears and the blood that gushed!

In the name of the our growing bellies,
Batons, buggers and bastards rife,
Let us revel in parades, lowering the emblem
Of the precious bones long lain asleep.

Amen!

6. *If Chiuta Were Man*
(Inspired by Malawian creation myths)

I. *The Soft Landing*

Woman, hold my shoulders
We'll drift and drift until
We reach the promised Nsinja
Forest and river of life.

When our safari is done,
We'll tell all animals and
Chiuta of our soft landing
Imploring them to follow suit.

Meanwhile, hold on woman,
Let's glide and glide
On our pioneer project –
Hope is our only hope.

II. *The First Fire*

Hard wood upon soft wood twirling
Sparks a sudden riot of mother and babies.

Corrosive flames devour Nsinja Forest
Chiuta's abode belches and blazes.

When frenzied lions storm out, jackals
Crackle gaping at man's invention.

The stampede thus whacked thuds away
Free from the hissing eggshells.

Only dogs, tails between legs,
Cower under the Man's fiery arm.

III. On Chiuta's Ascension

When you disgruntled spiralled
On spider's frail thread
Swearing you'd see us die to feel
The pain of our own invention,

When you thundering angry voices
That still send us scurrying for
Shelter promised your urine to save us
From our unquenchable fire,

When you on your multi-coloured
Bow on Ntiwa Hill declared
You'd stop your bleeding urine
If we did not improve,

Why, Chiuta, scampering on
Spider's thread to your Ivory Tower,
Why didn't you also warn
Our eyes would forever be smoky?

IV. So God Became A Chameleon

A muezzin
With gelded
Tongue
Slunk in
Celibacy

A politician
Empiric
Muffing
Easy balls
Fearing fear

V. The Tussle

And so Son
Next time you are
On sand playing animal
Play not hyena carried
Away by lion rather
The lion;
If forced
Carry him away
Make the hyena that
Killed the lion,
When he grumbles
Tell him it's only
A game – animal game
You are men and
He'll lead the next
Chick-stealing
Pig-blood-tapping
Party anyway.
You've seen
The latest
Tussle!

7. Song Of Chickens

Master, you talked with bows,
Arrows and catapults once
Your hands steaming with hawk blood
To protect your chicken.

Why do you talk with knives now,
Your hands teaming with eggshells
And hot blood from your own chicken?
Is it to impress your visitors?

8. The Sweet Brew At Chitakale

The old woman squats before a clay jar of *thobwa*
She uncovers the basket lid from the jar and
Stirs attention with a gourdful of the brew.

The customers have all been here: cyclists
In dripping sweat have deposited their coins
In the basket gulping down their share,

Pedestrians on various chores have talked
Before the exchange and then cooled their
Parched throats to their money's worth,

But this bus passenger bellows for a gourdful
From the window, drinks deliberately slowly until
The conductor presses the go-button –

The woman picks up the pieces of her broken
Gourd, and dusting her bottom, again squats
Confronting her brew with a borrowed cup.

9. *The Glorious Past*

Those women with tattoos on their navels
Beads around their waists and *zipini*
On their noses, those women on leopard
Skins surrounded by greased gourds
Snuff on their palms and sneezing their
Brilliant past to whoever they could
Honour or gurgling their past mysteries
From their bedecked hookahs –
                            Can they be
These women in plastic bangles
Coughing in broken proverbs
Rejoicing their son is back
The village is blessed and appealing
In the name of our politeness why can't I
Toss another calabash of *masese* beer
Before we together unravel
The story of our precious glorious past?

10. *These Too Are Our Elders*

Watch these elders; they always come at night
In bloated plumage, tossing you on their
Avocado noses, inhaling all the free air out
Of you; their masks carry fatal viruses.

One came the other night draped in hyena skins
His face showing amid the fluffed out ostrich
Feathers, twisting his sinews in a frenzied
Dance. At work I was unseating him, he preached.

But I too went to the village he had visited.
They said I should ask him next time why
He always came at night, why he pretended
I was more useful than the white man once in

My seat, and why he sent me to school at all?
Well, he merely backslid through the bamboo rafters
Showering behind rotten amulets and mice shit!
Why do these elders always exploit our disbelief?

Epitaph For A Mad Friend

(For Joe Masinga)

Do you remember in Mtendere buses
Stopping at Ulongwe to replenish,
Through bus windows to poke curry-fried-chicken
In urchin basins below, chewing, content,
Joking about the man who ties the rains each year?

Do you remember my mad friend standing
Suddenly there, paw-paw juice streaking down
His front from yester crop, and then
The tatters mockingly imploring:
Andwanje suwa siwili, ambe likobili!*

Don't you remember the passengers roaring
With laughter and tears, and you turning to me:
'How dare I hit him twice on his head for my penny?'
And brushing, cruising on in hiccups down
The dusty road to the lake?

But on the eve of our eleventh independence
Today, after the beautiful tarmac to the lake
And my brief spell abroad,
I hear Mercy warn:
'Even Andwanje-suwa-siwili is gone!'

**ChiYao for 'Hit me twice on the head and give me
a penny for it.'*

On His Royal Blindness
Paramount Chief Kwangala

I admire the quixotic display of your paramountcy,
How you brandish our ancestral shields and spears
Among your warriors dazzled by your loftiness,
But I fear the way you spend your golden breath;
Those impromptu, long-winded tirades of your might
In the heat, do they suit your brittle constitution?

I know I too must sing to such 'royal' happiness
And I am not arguing. Wasn't I too tucked away
In my loin-cloth infested by jiggers and fleas before
Your bright eminence showed up? How could I quibble
Over your having changed all that? How dare I when
We have scribbled our praises all over our graves?

Why should I quarrel when I too have known mask
Dancers making troubled journeys to the gold mines
On bare feet, bringing back fake European gadgets –
The broken pipes, torn coats, crumpled bowler hats,
Dangling mirrors and rusty tin-cans to make their
Mask dancing strange? Didn't my brothers die there?

No, your grace, I am no alarmist nor banterer, I am
Only a child surprised how you broadly disparage me
Shocked by the tedium of your continuous palaver. I
Adore your majesty. But paramountacy is like a raindrop
On a vast sea. Why should we wait for the children to
Tell us about our toothless gums or our showing flies?

In Memory Of Matthew, 1976

You should have gone down with malaria
I'd have brought you those *nakatobwa* mangoes
You so much cherished,

We'd have joked about the mosquitoes
We once smoked to death with acacia leaves –
Chattering kids picking each other's lice,

I'd have told you about the squirrel
We caught stealing cabbage
In our backyard garden the other day;

And that pear-seedling
You took to transplant,
Why didn't you allow it to sprout?

The House That Florrie Intended

She was building a stone house here once
To match with the times, she carelessly declared
Selecting her slabs and passing them on to
Her husband to lay the foundation. Young
Abu and Jemu playing cork-float beach-ball
Rolled on the fine dry sands of Koko Bay,
Edi and Lizi washing their cassava to dry
In the hot sun, caught little fish in their
Bamboo baskets screeching in joy and triumph;
And on this tablet of rock I sat half-nude,
I remember hatching a little revolution with
Myself, brooding on an arched life, my arms
Cupping the chin, the brow tensed, the legs
Crossed, watching the endless blue waters of
The vast lake curl, break, lap-lapping at my
Feet as the minnows nibbled at my toes. Then
A loin-cloth fisherman, emerging from the men
Bent mending their broken nets under the shade
Of the lone beach-tree, jumped into a canoe
Fettered to a nearby colony of reeds and grass,
He sculled away lazily perhaps to check the night's
Fish-traps. Meanwhile, beyond those rocks that
Drill in bird-shit like breasts in white bras or
Two eggshells, a sharp fish-eagle lingering
Swooped down for his afternoon *chambo*. And
Florrie passed on the morning's last stone to
Ibrahim. What transpired after that, I cannot tell
Except that I dared briefly abroad and I gather
Florrie & Ibrahim witnessed in protest; I hear her
Radiogram, the rumba records the kids so much
Cherished, their spring beds and mattresses and
The fridge, spoons and forks too witnessed her

Departure. And today when Florrie's kids stand
Desperate at my embarrassed door, I've come to see
The straggling cornerstones of her house intended.

Handshakes And Best Wishes, 1972

Late. The heat of September afternoons
Pours hardening your face, cracking your lips;
Airport hustle, hubbub, bags and bag slips;
In the balcony above, the disciples toss
To expected final handshakes and best wishes
But their zealous hands must falter as a rush
Hand nervously alarms towards the runway –
Sentence: Oh, well … go drink from the source!

In truth there had been enough handshakes –
The village neighbour cursing his son for
'Getting out of the school window, shaming me!'
The Chief with a bubbling calabash hoping
His best wishes brought back ever-flowing calabashes,
The girl-cousin declaring another marriage postponed –
'A rabbit must have run between your legs, you!'
And mother's dry twig pecking at the sere earth, quiet.

The handshakes and best wishes were many and
As we are spared more today: the choking gossip
And the extravagant pomp and speeches – even
The captain's beaten apology for the delay at
Entebe as Idi Amin issues the pass, releases.

Sketches Of London

The source: flaming cardboard boxes with squeaking
Staircases. Like smoked cockroaches we sneak out
Of peeling caches; the conduits bleak behind plate
Glass; the concrete blocks grey, unmoved – the brush
Won't do. Plastic litterbags burst open drip in mews,
Poodle's muck on pavements, the ladies don't mind;
Refuse collectors went on strike weeks and weeks ago –
Glory be! Whoever said there was a fountain here?

The Serpentine: a lovely recreation but if they had
Mosquitoes here this city would be a desert. Thames
Banks: they picked up a dead woman the other day,
Her lungs were found wrapped up in World War soot,
She must have been living here thirty years, they said.
The Tower: King Henry's abattoirs; his wives' regalia
Still trail amid the steaming guillotines,
The bathtubs are meticulously kept for ten pence.

I knew a playful priest once back home
I was always late for his catechism lessons
He gave me three strokes to show me the way
He said, but the cane snapped before the fourth,
In anger he threw away the broken pieces
And instead touched the little thing between
My legs. Didn't I giggle, running away!

The First Train To Liverpool
(Enfield: Liverpool 1, Stoke 0, 1972)

(A Letter for Angela)

No last minute haggling about prices
Of curry – chicken first at Balaka
No stinking Afro-wigs into your mouths
No leaping from bags of peanuts into
Baskets of tomato, cheerfully quarrelling
Nor finally sitting on half a buttock;
Euston Station contacts and dialogues
Through wires and innumerable papers
Only comfort welcomes aboard a sudden silence
That soon reigns, our eyes weighing and
Quickly avoiding each other between
The beverages and the local papers.

Runcorn Station welcomes aboard a haunting
Quiet where men obviously build more paper
Walls against other men. No curios, no mats,
No herbs sell through windows. No mothers
Suckle their crying babies. No jokes about
The rains held up by your charms this year!
At Lime Street itself, not even a drunk staggers
Out perhaps to announce his newly acquired
Cornerstones. Only recorded voices bid you
Come again before the engulfing impenetrable
Crowds. But the maddening quiet soon recedes
Locating a bright tarnished face once known.

Travelling In London Tubes

(For VSOs, 1973, Childs Hall, Reading University)

There is something funny about
The dust back home
The way it blows
Naively with the wind
And carelessly settles
On flowers and maize gardens
Blemishing the green;
The way it rolls
Behind the big cars on the dusty roads
Like cotton wool ashed
Leaving you rubbing your eyes
Like a child;
Yet you can avoid it all so easily too
Just keep your head up, above,
Or even laugh
And let the big cars pass.

But here, even the dust is subtle,
The way it blows
With the seemingly fresh breeze
And settles
On your window-sill
In your eyes
And nose,
Even the dust is subtle here.

And it is not until the day is out,
If you should stand at your window
Facing the breeze apparently blowing cool,
It is not until your sudden
Aitchoo!

That you begin to see how much
Charcoal was in your nose
Eyes
Lungs
Travelling in those lovely tubes.

A Letter From Florrie Abrahim Witness, Fort Mlangeni, Mocambique, December, 1972

There are times when their faiths in gods
Really fascinates me. Take when the Anglican
Priest with all pomp and ceremony married
Abrahim and Florrie, why didn't he realise
Abe and Florrie would eventually witness
The true Jehovah in his most pristine? And silly
Little Florrie, couldn't she foresee the run against
The only Cards possible when she said her
'Yes, I do, for kids or for none?' And when
Florrie's mother, dear, with all her Anglican
Limping love for her first and only daughter
Still intact, even when she thought she might
Still visit the prodigals notwithstanding, how
Couldn't she see she too would be booted out
– Landing carelessly bruised, and in Moca-
mbique! The buggers! They surely deserve it!
They deserve such a good kick on their bottom.
I mean, there are times when their faith just
Fails me. Take today, when silly little Florrie
Should scribble a funny epistle on stupid roll –
And Love, did you have to call it thus? I mean,
It sounds so strangely imprudent of … But …
Anyway: Darling Brother, only God of Abraham
Knows how we escaped the petrol and matches
Yet we are all in good hands. They give us
Free flour, beans free and their kind of salted
Meat and fish. 'We've even built a ten-by-ten yard
Little hospital for our dear selves'. Only we
Haven't got any soap. But we'll manage and do not
Be anxious over us here dear Brother; Mummy

And the kids are all in good shape. They send
Their Christmas greetings. Read well and oh, note:
Psalms! Where is London is the blooming Bible?

Drinking The Water From Its Source

Distancing ourselves now our metaphors sharpen
We say 'drink the water from its source' naively
Probably thinking of its purity, our salvation
Or the dead empire. We know only too well that
All water springs from sources so inscrutable
Yet drinking water far from the sources we often
Exalt our images heedless of the minor details:
Streams gather debris from antique sunspots
Depositing the silt onto infinite sand-beds;
The gliding Shire River mystifies us watering
Our golden lives, and tantalized we then conclude
The source of the waters must be more exotic.

But drinking the water from its source is like
A prayer: after we have slipped out of our
Sandals washing our grey feet for the moment
We only seek the point of our troubled voices
Hoping thereby to reassemble our broken confidence
We know that after the prayer we'll slip back
Into our sandals buckling more dust, probing
Greater salvation, again watching the hour when
The muezzin should raise his voice for another
Congregation. Drinking the water from the 'sources'
We must turn back to the peripheral mosaics of home
Revealing the depth of their natural negatives.

As The West End Allegro Subsides Today

(For Landeg White, 1975)

When you went on about those Trinidadian
Steel Bands and calypso in your Chichiri flat
I did not really care; I nodded only out of
Goodwill nor did I expect the winds to blow
Us into another flat on Chepstow Road
And one London summer afternoon watch
The whole carnival, colourful, brisk, gently
Flowing towards Notting Hill Gate
Graced by tuneful steel bands as baby
Martin watching cricket on TV pulled out
The plugs fidgeting about being left alone
To learn to crawl. But as the West End
Allegro subsides today and the periodic
Blurt of Zomba muezzins carelessly mingles
With the croaking crows of Chirunga
Estate to consummate our re-entry into
An otherwise cautious quiet green, tempers
Often fray – shouldn't I have cared at all?

Visiting Zomba Plateau

Could I have come back to you to wince
Under the blur of your negatives,
To sit before braziers without the glow
Of charcoal, to cringe at your rivers
That without their hippos and crocs
Merely trickle gratingly down, to watch
Dragonflies that no longer fascinate and
Puff adders that have lost their puff?
Where is your charming hyena tail –
Praying mantis who cared for prayers once?
Where is the spirit that touched the hearts
Lightly – chameleon colours of home?
Where is your creation myth? Have I come
To witness the carving and jingling only of
Your bloated images and piddling mirrors?

Re-entering The Shrines Of Zomba

At the gates the guardians have set up cockroaches and
Leeches to protect the shrines from stray iconoclasts

The tax-collectors ominously wink at each other
Weighing the genuineness of your travellers cheques

The secretaries titillate freely about their bastards
Watching your first syllables. The gods have deserted

These noble shrines. A new religion is born. And
When the sacrificial hour arrives, the custodians first

Surrender to the deception of demijohns, then gyrating
To rhythms of mystic drums, they shovel their satchels

Of neuroses onto the sacred rocks and bow. They seek no
Advice how to bring back willing old gods; so the rains

Won't come; the rueful lambs refuse to bleat at the altars
And in the grottoes benumbed virgins put out the candles.

Glory Be To Chingwe's Hole

(The ChiNyanja version of the Greek myth of 'Pygamalion'.)

Chingwe's Hole, you devoured the Chief's prisoners
Once, easy villagers decked in leopard colours
Pounding down their energies and their sight;
You choked minstrel lovers with wild granadilla
Once, rolling under burning flamboyant trees.

Do you remember Frog the carver carving Ebony Beauty,
Do you remember Frog's pin on Ebony Beauty's head
That brought Ebony to life. And when the Chief
Heard of Beauty betrothed to Frog, whose dogs
Beat up the bushes to claim Ebony for the Chief?

Even when Fly alarmed Frog of the impending hounds,
Who cracked Fly's bones? Chingwe's Hole, wood –
peckers once poised for vermilion strawberries merely
Watched fellow squirrels bundled up in sacks
Alive as your jaws gnawed at their brittle bones.

Chingwe's Hole, how dare I praise you knowing whose
Marrow still flows in murky Namitembo River below?
How dare I raise my voice knowing what will happen?
You strangled our details boasting your plush dishes,
Dare I glorify your rope and depth epitomising horror?

Gerrie's Season of Goodwill, 1975

(For Lan White, Jim Stewart, Robin Graham & other deportees)

When Gerrie flew in to teach early this year we
Introduced him to the Lower House of the Gymkhana
Club. But the pub's effigy, papier-mâché Queen
Victoria amused him immensely. How could she
Still have the nerve to preside over the raffle of silver
Trophies, expatriates, bartenders, the few mortals –
The stalwart mess? He asked. Everyone was startled
By Gerrie's naivety and his daring admission that
He'd never played golf in his life, that the expats
Silly gossip or their exchange of tennis or bridge
Partners for life or the locals' forever gloating
About their undeclared polygamies, bored him stiff.
But before we could allow Gerrie more enthusiastic
Words: that he'd come for a bit of the local culture
Really or for bottle walking! which was dangerous
As he'd already gathered from the reliable rumours,
Sapato, our local authority on Gerrie's kind, butted
In with, 'Just the sort for this year's Squash Trophy!'
Ordering, of course, the fourth round of drinks. Well,
You can imagine what happens after such a start:
Round after round after pub after boiled eggs after
Laughter until Gerrie, of course, summoned up enough
Courage to go it alone. Well, yesterday, didn't we have
To see Gerrie off, briefly? And when his neighbours
Subtly declared, 'You shouldn't have been so naughty
Really, you know; breaking other people's laws
Deserves imprisonment back home, remember?'
Gerrie's wife offered them the Victorian bamboo chair
And the kids' games they could not pack. And Gerrie
Himself joked carelessly, 'I was only here for the beer!'

Hounds In Puddles

The hounds were out again last week
Scaring the children playing ball in puddles outside

One child had a very bad trip
The hounds nearly mauled him to death

Wasn't I nervous!

Last night a bluebill sparrow strayed into
Our crowded living room

The light blinded her to roost
The children laughed almost crushing her to death

Didn't my blood well!

It's been like this these sensitive years, you see,
With bits of smoke issuing under *nsolo* trees,

But soon, I know,

The green hounds will maul these tender children
And the children the crispy sparrows

And I shudder.

Waiting For The Electronic Forceps

(For Felix Mnthali taken at 3.30 am)

Michael, your prayer for the butterfly
Clutched between your warm fingers
That the Lord might still grant her
A distant sense of humour with the Sun
Or the bright colours of her wings
Despite the garbage breath of this earth,
Your prayer was strained.

                    And whoever took
Seriously drunken Presbyters or toothless
Shepherds who fear to undertake their
Precious sheep lost in cold abattoirs?
Not even the Sun itself now, I imagine,
When your handcuffed butterfly sprawls
In the freezing dark walls – waiting
For the electronic pins and forceps!

The Plane Tree In Talbot Square

(A Letter to David Kerr & Lavinia Spencer, December 1976)

The moral of the plane tree in Talbot Square
How it braces the seasons and tells our time

Your cheerless grey sky matching the concrete walls
The Londoner's wink of the eye and tilt of the head

Our type of communication

Your blues with the homebrew bitter at Purfleet
Reflecting demented Dracula house opposite

Even the publisher's patron tone on our type
Of verse at John and Gizzy's wine and cheese

Today, these tenuous memories strangely tighten.

      And dear Lavinia,
Today I recall our Paddington Tube Station nerves

Of a bomb happily defused

And your Moscow souvenir cigars I left unkindly
In the black plastic litterbag outside the door

For as the golden sun went down on us
Today another comrade went in

And did my heart jump!

The familiar landscapes and banal images of home
For whom the lips falsely part

Blur.

We Wondered About The Mellow Peaches

(After the arrest of the notorious Malawi Congress Party's secretary
general and administrative secretary, Albert Muwalo, for
supposedly plotting to assassinate Banda)

So, behind the heavy backyard orchard
And your generous invitations, Alberto,
To guava tart today and mango pudding tomorrow
Behind the spate of those Chilobwe township
Lambs brutally chopped in their dark huts
Where even undertakers dare not tread,
                                        There
Were whiskers, Alberto, to map the moves
And pay the bills? Why, why did I waste my
Melodious song excoriating parochial squirrels
And hammerheads for readily running messages
Up and down bowing peach trees and bringing
Flashy girls with mellow peaches and vermilion
Strawberries into lascivious range-rovers?
I should have set up votive slabs from Mphunzi
Hills, chalked the rude walls with gentle
Gazelles and the lore about sweet foundlings –
To while away my temper. And yet, how could
The chameleon have lost grip of his own colours?
And did we need the restive decades to uncover
The plot? And this fuss about conspiracies and goats,
Didn't we all wonder about the mellow peaches?

April 1978, The Prisoners Quietly Back

For goodness sake Sweetie, let's stop fretting
About turbid top cockroaches without the brains
To penetrate even their own images. Let us
For once, when the prisoners are quietly home,
Enjoy the fruits of the evergreen landscape of
Zomba plateau. Let us walk up this Colossus
When the winding avenues are littered with
The purple of jacarandas and the tongues of
Flames-of-the-forests.

                    At the sawmill let us
Pause to greet plateau boys buying their fresh
Luscious granadilla and gorgeous strawberries
And up Mlungusi fountain let us select a rock
To sit down on, and as the sparrows hop about
The tree branches twittering, let us chew our
Chambo sandwiches to the welling crests splattering
Nervously down the river. Or let us fondle our
Released hope hurtling down the turf in a strange
Joy today when the prisoners are quietly back.

Nor Will I Believe The Glorious Retreat

*(Reply to a letter from Ian Michael: I thought you'd all crack up after
your endless et cetera, but obviously you've survived the ...)*

If you ask me Michael, today even Angela thought
She too might streak in the heat of our pointless
Monotonous ranting; so fuming about the et cetera
She ran up Mulungusi River and on a prodigious rock
Collapsed sweltering under a purpling jacaranda
The deep-blue-purple flowers rained cool on her
Like pigeons at Trafalgar Square once, she boasted;
And as suddenly those squirrels and cockroaches
That gnawed at our precious nerves and private
Cabbages fossilized into a silly joke,
And those beleaguered decades without a smile or
Shame retreated, leaving behind dewed Carlsbergs
And beaming samusas for the pick. But you know how I
Read time when she should take her stock so starkly
Naively; don't I still remember how cockroaches
And squirrels breed, how could I believe their
Retreat? But for once even Angela who never really
Talks, carelessly said: I think I'll go shit on
The road tomorrow and tell the retreat that I have
Sinned grossly; I'm sure Father Patrick will heartily
Ask me to count my beaded Carlsbergs by the tens!

At The Metro: Old Irrelevant Images, 1979

(For Blaise Machila)

They are still so anthropologically tall here,
Still treating you in irrelevant tribal metaphors:
Somalis have softer skins, they drink milk, they say
(And yours is cracking, you drink *kachasu*!*)

Even the most knowledgeable still slip back
Apologising to you in banal Tarzan images:
The children still know mostly Tarzans at school, they say
(Tarzans choked me too in the fifties, damn it!)

But University College London girls' sit-in about rapists
Was a bit of a change, and Mrs Thatcher's et cetera
Against overseas students and, the publisher's dinner!
(How are the jacarandas I left blooming, otherwise?)

*Locally distilled gin

On Being Asked To Write A Poem For 1979

Without kings and warriors occasional verse fails;
Skeletal Kampuchia children staring, cold,
Stubborn Irish children throwing grenades –
These are objects too serious for verse;
Crushed Soweto children clutching their entrails
Then in verse bruised, mocks.

Today no poet sufficiently asks why dying children
Stare or throw bombs. And why should we
Compute painful doubts that will forever occupy us?
Talking oil-crises in our eight cylinder cars
Is enough travesty ...

The year of the child must make no difference then
Where tadpoles are never allowed to grow into frogs!

From
*The Chattering Wagtails
of Mikuyu Prison* (1993)

Of Our Chiefs And Their Concubines, 1981

Last Christmas they sat beside the hearths
Secure, together, cracking roast chestnuts

Or stale jokes about holies and ivies
As red wines cooled down another hot year

Today, even the vines threaten to stream
The streets with banners of another fire.

Out Of Bounds (Or Our Maternity Asylum)

I was out of bounds, they insisted, outside
The wards, where iron roof crumble under

Rotting *mlombwa* leaves, green paint rusts
To two decades of dead dust, windows are

Covered in threads of matting (to stop our
Scorpion pneumonia of June?) Inside, some

Sixty inmates of spasming women top & tail
On thirty beds, ninety others with infants

Scramble over the cracked cold cement floor –
A family under each bed, most in between.

On a slab, a cramped enamel plate (with
A piece of tripe she could not chew) labours

But this is no asylum & no one is fighting
The desert war here. These are refugees only

From 'Child Spacing', atoning for the ghost
Revolution twenty years ago, repaired in this

Shrinking hospital God knows how. And I gather
The doctors & nurses who toil twenty-four hours

(With blunt needles, without drugs, on a small
Wage) offered to extend this wing: there was

The usual hiccup about 'official clearance'
Yet this was the rallying cry of the dais once

Upon a time. And when the powers visit
The sick at Christmas, some caesareans will be

Prematurely discharged, others jostled into
Neat lines, clapping their praises. The windows

Will have been glazed, the blood bespattered
Walls painted. They'll borrow beds & canvases

From the nearby hospital so Father Christmas
Sees one patient per bed: another dream done!

But I hear, I am out of bounds?

Kadango Village, Even Milimbo Lagoon Is Dry

(for Landeg & Alice, 1981)

In the cracking heat of October, our village market;
A queue of skeletal hands reaching out for the last
Cowlac tin of loose grain, falters, against all hope;

In the drought, a frail dog sniffing his lover's arse
Goes berserk, barking at the wave of grey eddying
Between the mountain boulders and the shrivelling lake;

Scurvy children kicking the grit, scud beach-wards,
Their wobbly feet digging in for possible cassava
Where even such tubers are now hushed in shoot.

Rocky geckos, blue tongues hanging out, scuttle on
The hot sand but biltong, belly up, before the beach;
Fish eagles suspended, swoop down for grasshoppers;

Even Milimbo lagoon is dead, no oar dips in any
More; those fishermen who dreamt up better weather
Once, no longer cast their nets here, and their

Delightful bawdy songs to bait the droughts are
Cloaked in the choking fumes of dawn, banned. But
Our fat-necked custodians despatch another tale.

When the Shire Valley dries up patiently (or The Last of the Sweet Bananas)

(for Megan Vaughan)

The crime is how we deliberately keep out of touch,
Pretending it has nothing to do with us, we've been
Through it all. Baobab fruit and grilled mice on clay plate,
How familiar the metaphors, we think, suspecting our
House servants of having killed and eaten our pet cats!
We do not feel the green mangoes drying up in the sun
Outside or the lorries festering in the backyards. And
When the naked women crowded at the village borehole
Begin knocking pails of water off each other's heads,
We wonder what the fight is about, those funny drunks!
At the University, expatriate lecturers will gesticulate,
Finger the leaves of Marx to a batch of yawning students,
Nervously trying to define something or other, their
Wives cheerfully wiping their bums on local News
After *nsima* dishes! Going local gently, they cautiously
Chide. But like the jacarandas we blossom indifferently
As our bank governors gravely worry about, 'These free
Japanese TV offers, Honourable Minister, should we
Really introduce them into the villages now, do you think?'
Colonies of storks in flamboyant trees look down on
The valley dust and the last of the sweet bananas.

The Farms That Gobble The Land At Home*

The farms peacefully chew up the land at home
Bulldozing docile mud huts, flattening broken
Reed shacks into neatly developed cakes, scatter-
ing their goats, chickens, pigeons or mice in
The swirling sand which blinds the eyes at home.
One farmer gather smaller farmers into WETs
(Wage-Earning-Tenants) offering them 30 coins
Per day, stopping their mixed planting, cheap
Original ashes and compost manure are banned
(To maximise profits) and fertilisers (only farms
Can afford) imposed. Men no longer need the mines
For gold, even women become breadwinners (with
Specially planned female wages to ensure their
Domestic sweat is not impaired) on the land our
Fathers fought for us back home. Moonlight drums
Fireside yarns are ripped under the auspices of
Rural Growth Centres and Recreations (such as
Whoring) carefully instituted to breed foreign
Exchange (for our guns, droughts and videos).
But when it rains, kindly, the snails still drag
Along their shells, the frogs hop about their
Monotonous stalls; only they mustn't croak about
Their daily dregs or the pesticides which blacken
Their skins and corrode their lungs, lest huge blue
Or green caterpillars on patrol crush them. So when
You walk about, only Peace & Calm Law & Order
Prevails on the fields that gobble the land at home.

*After the Ghanaian poet, Kofi Awoonor.

The Haggling Old Woman At Balaka

The old woman at Balaka never stops
She haggles over every new event:

'I was fed on breasts and goat milk
Not on your silly, dust-milk-tins!
And you girls of today are cocked up,
You sell chicken eggs for cokes and fantas
To suckle your babies, then you ask me
Why your babies are rickets and ribs?

'Now you come to lend me money, you say,
To buy fertilisers to improve my yield –
How generous, how degrading! And I must
Suppose your banks won't dry out! Can't
You see I am too tired for these tricks?

'And from now on I will keep my crop to
Myself – you have no shame building your
Brick houses on old women's dying energies
Under the lie of your national development!
No, I've sung too many tattered praises,
Spare me these spotted desires, children …'

Dear granny at Balaka fidgets too much
– I fear for what she'll brag about next.

Vigil For A Fellow Credulous Captive

(For Anenenji & other unsung heroes and heroines)

Someday, perhaps he too will come back home,
Not like a lion avenging his muzzle once shattered
Nor a cheetah stalking his long awaited prey –
No dead bones, however tough, ever take on flesh
Again, outside myths. No, someday Anenenji will
Surface as bones, mere bones, brittly washed up this
Makokola beach, scattered by the morning breakers
Of this gentle lake. And the rough sack they shoved
Him in will drift along in shreds, perhaps hanging
Delicately to a yellowing drove of water-lilies or
Some sudd, forgotten, the heavy millstone once on his
Legs having broken free. Only then will it probably
Dawn on us to cast our mask and gather those frosty
Mornings he spent picking tea for a weekly handful
Of cheerless, foggy tickies; those blistering afternoons
He clambered up distant craggy hills to sell Party Cards
– A credulous captive to some dreamer's dementia!
From door to door coercing, like one venting his displaced
Rut, sometimes thrice in season, insisting every baby
Bought a Party Card: for the market, the bus, life …
What moved him, what his wife saw, you could not guess;
Not even once when you, feverishly bemused by all this
Fuss of only a mortal against other mortals, tracked
The splintered bare-feet chugging homeward with a full
Purse to the area Party Headquarters or watched those
Cracked hands rolling coils of brown tobacco, puffing
And rescuing by the tail a maimed lizard dropped from
The cobweb bamboo rafters; not after sharing his pop maize
For dinner even, could you tell what he really cared for
And why. But today, a mute wife before a crushed paraffin
Tin-can lamp keeps vigil over Anenenji's fireplace, alone.

Nobody, no mound or tombstone stands to say where
Or what justice he might have suffered. Perhaps someday
He'll come again with another pack of Cards to sell,
Menacing!

Baobab Fruit Picking
(Or Development In Monkey Bay)

(For David & Mary Kerr)

'We've fought before, but this is worse than rape!'
In the semi-Sahara October haze, the raw jokes

Of Balamanja women are remarkable. The vision
We revel in has sent their husbands to the mines

Of Jo'burg, to buy us large farms, she insists.
But here, the wives survive by their wits & sweat –

Shoving dead cassava stalks into rocks, catching
Fish in tired *chitenje* cloths with kids, picking

Baobab fruit & whoring. The bark from the baobab
Trunk they strip into strings for their reed wattle,

The fruit they crack, scoop out the white, mix with
Goat milk, 'That's porridge for today, children!'

The shell is drinking gourd or firewood split
(They used to grate the hard cores into girls'

Initiation oil once). 'But you imported the Boers
Who visited our Chiefs at dawn, promising boreholes!

These pine cottages on the beach shot up instead, some
With barbed wire fences fifty yards into the lake!'

(What cheek!) Now each weekend, 'the blighted-tomato-
thighs in reeking loin-cloths' come, boating, grinning

At them baobab fruit picking. 'My house was right
Here!' Whoever dares check these Balamanja dreamers!

Moving Into Monkey Bay
(With Pioneer Charcoal Sellers)

After their pine beach cottages
Moving into Balamanja North blunders,

No monkey beckons to you under
The dappled shade of palm-trees,

No one hacks the occasion free with
Phangas, Balamanja North is bush

Still to be priced; only sandwiches
& beer grace the take-over bid.

A canoe. Timorous hands after years
Without oars. In the gloaming breeze

The bay drifts with blue-knotted
Water-lilies, brown leaves rotting

& decayed baobab fruit entangle in
The sudd contrasting the live shells

On the shore. But how do bull-frogs
Come to grief among dragonflies here?

The canoe cannot pass. The oar's dip
Releases a throng of anopheles. Note,

We have company: after belching with
Sacks of charcoal & finding steel bolts

The gates of his prospective buyer,
After trudging back to his tin-roof

Hovel & perhaps a brisk quarrel with
His wife, who should picnic his desires

On my bay? I shoo the mosquitoes &
Row in.

Flying Over The Summer Haze Of Home

(For Lupenga Mphande & Frank Chipasula, 1983/84)

Why is our African summer often unsettling,
Why must flying over home sink the heart?

In Rwanda we joked about their proto-Bantu
Beer but their dense proto-drought was not

Amusing hanging thus like industrial dust
On faceless banana fronds whittling them;

Swaziland smogs Queen of Sheba's breasts
Reducing eminent witch-doctors into trackers

Of prostitute ghosts beside Mbabane cliffs
After their devouring cyclone domoina. Outside

Harare, Domboshawa crickets shriek in dry
Monotones. And the fierce lions of Nairobi,

Lean from the heat of the National Park, road-
block the airport highway to bemused tourist

Shutters. Even from these heights of Ku Chawe
Inn of Zomba Plateau, no army tanks lumber in

Or out of Chingwe's Hole below, no visiting
Seasoned German pilot dares hang-glide his

Way down this tough brown tissue as onerous
Army-worms nibble at the last of the green leaves.

We bored our way through nameless thickets
Of cloud above hoping for the rains below,

But secretly fearing we'd merely sit and note
Stinking dung-beetles pushing their lot into

Chingwe's Hole (with no charm to foretell our
Rains in this world without a horizon). And

When does this haze intend to lift? Sometimes
It feels like you are watching mountain fires

Just contained or a huge down-pour of December
Rains is at hand, perhaps finally here! But no, it's

Another October, arid and hot and somewhere
In that ubiquitous haze another babe will drop.

Burning The Witch For The Rains
(The Dark Case)

(For Fr Pat O'Malley)

Is this perhaps the last of our dear sluts, this
Witch frowning vacantly, condemned only

By her snuff-black gums & the stark veins?
When did matriarchal bones living in rotten

Thatch hatchback become a menace, people?
& does she muse upon her grimy shroud or

The bane of our brittle existence? Malignant
Village vigilantes stack up dry acacia twigs

& brambles, smarting for the witch's fire
After our cheek flaying, head shaving ritual;

The stern omnipotent hand uncovers the official
Evidence: exhibit one, an amorphous dark case,

She's supposed to have locked up lighting
& thunder so the rains don't come. When one

Zealot opened the case at the police station, the box's
Bowels growled like bloodhounds, blinding him

(The curious jury of kids bends with laughter);
Exhibit two: the bag of fertiliser she stole,

The malcontent apparently still believes in her
Mixed planting with ashes & compost manure –

Dare the rebellious dreadlocks resist as barking
Youth-leaguers dive for their bloody antic rites ...?

The Rise Of The New Toadies, May 1983*

(For Felix Mnthali)

The streaming blood of luscious Zomba strawberries
Coagulates today. A cold spell overcasts this plateau

No cheeky lads hop about with granadilla basketfuls,
No black Mercedes slitshers about the compounds below

Road blocks. The silent megaphone blurts, 'Any more
Yobbos try their liberal jokes again, gun-point burial,

No undertakers. We police your keyholes, jam your foreign
Radios. No bishop fidgets about requiem masses: church-gates

Char. Otherwise, village exit visas for 'rebel' presbyters,
The self-imposed curfew starts at seven, beyond that

Everybody sniffs from the backyard of their fuming huts –
To spare the people further slanderous outside lies …'

Apparently, the 'yobbos' only wanted the air cleared, but
The other toadies wouldn't wait – you know the pattern!

*Composed after the murder, as instructed by Banda and his 'inner
circle', of popular politicians Aaron Gadama, Dick Matenje, David
Chiwanga & Twaibu Sangala.*

No, Creon, There's No Virtue In Howling

'It is no glory to kill and kill again.' Teiresias in Antigone.

No, Creon, you overstate your image to your
People. No, there's no virtue in howling so.
How can you hope to repair Haemon, your
Own blood, our only hope for the throne,
By reproaching his body mangled by your
Decree and put to rest without the requiem
Of our master drums? What tangential sentries
Advise you to bemoan the dead by scoffing at
Them publicly thus? Those accidents your
Flunkies master-stroked, those tortures &
Exiles fashioned, and the blood you loved
To hear, did we need more lies? Look now,
Even the village lads toss their coins for old
Creon's days. What cowardice, what perversity
Grates life-laden minds on our death-beds?

Easter Apologies For Babble Dreams

(To My Wife, 1983)

You dreamt of a room of your own
With mother's ostrich-neck clay jars
(Decked in mystic beads and triangles)
Shaping the four corners and lianas
From them straying up the ceiling;

You hoped for the delicate carves of
Village ladles and wood masks and
Home gourds the children would paint
In Easter-egg colours, pendulous on
Your light-blue walls. Outside, you

Saw the jasmine sweetening the pears,
Peaches and the tender palm trees
So that if I needed metaphors, you
Teased, I should not have to patrol
The woods of Chingwe's Hole, shame-

lessly startling the squirrels on heat
Or the sparrows ministering to the rock
Owls snoring to the gentle splashes of
Mulungusi river; and if the children
Should want branches for Palm Sunday,

They'd merely run the backyard boughs
As we munched our paw-paw sandwiches.
But it was not to be, my dear, and if our joys
Had chanced by your dream, we'd probably
Have aggravated the children's asthma!

Smiller's Bar Revisited, May 1983

(For Anthony Nazombe)

No, how do you know they no longer seek what
Their hearts desire those girls at Smiller's Bar?

Note how they sneer at your dawns & bonfires
Now that you have accidentalised* their beloved

Combatants. And having known so many nebulous
Fleas, why shouldn't they claim vague memories

Of your so-called liberation struggle? And in this
Feminist age, grant them revised metaphors, man!

You can't be so sure your buttercups gather here
Only to scent down the few rebels their masters

(Mindless-brittle-neck-hackers!) still invent
For them, and what nonsense, what paranoia!

It's true at bar counters the masters lurch to your
Side, offering you round after round of beer,

Setting up their abandoned adulteresses for you
To settle on or their sadistic tales to respond to:

'That rhinoceros you gunned down scratching
His livid wounds on pepper wood, wasn't it fun

How he collapsed, twitching', they laugh hoping
You can join in the joke & be properly convicted!

But you must concede, after you accidentalised*
Their Anenenjis,† the nuance of your classical

Butterfly today slips away; even you don't know
Who the real master is when, from her creased

Victorian frock, she rectifies your change without
Blush & pontificates about inflation having

Trebled her price. Indeed, why should anybody's
Bastard at home eat the grass? So, give the girls

A break, let the coloured bulbs, the drunken moths
& robot drums choke the bay; who said freedom's

Not a bifurcated pig? Revisiting Smiller's Bar
May be the beginning of your true liberation!

*To accidentalise is to kill and pretend it was an accident when
everybody knows it was not (first used by the Writers' Group,
Chancellor College, University of Malawi, 1983 after the
assassination of Gadama and co).

†Anenenjis: public figures, never given the platform to air their
views, their crime is to believe in a constitution-fearing, non-
corrupt, just and free society.

For Fear Of Which Mandras Images & Which Death? (Or When The Nation Stood In Horror)

Clouds of adversity are gathering on the mountain
Tops; last Saturday, guerrillas overran Kapolo

Police Station lynching 3 constables, but the local
MP's news-clip stresses, 'It was only bandits & you

Still love me, anyway!' The radio cracks with
More callous trivia, shamelessly inventing new

Rebels for the gallows. When head-shaven hang-
man, vigilante-flanked, swoops in for his rites,

Nerves rack. Where & how did this village seize
Its chronic malaria that even quinine flowing

Into its veins by drip won't do? What miasma
Brought this cancerous growth that nobody wants

To broach for fear of death? We all know their
Bogus faces in the corridors, but when we pass

The Mandrax Images, we merely chuckle at the in-
ward truths we know we share but won't admit

For fear of dubbing each other liars. Even our
Snoop's metaphors are anaemic & scatty – the poor

Cockroach must be wondering now whether it was
Worth it, hiding those lonely tears of Chingale

Mother whose child was bellowed to death by
Breath of god's helicopter on earth. If the children

Still rudely ask about that lorry the women high –
jacked to their Party meeting, 'Whatever become

Of the protesting driver, as metal, woman & rock
Mangled down canyon?' If children wonder about

The Bibles & Eggs offered at altars every bumper
Rains, 'When do they multiply?' What of us, what

Incurable despair has gripped us that our lips
Won't open, for fear of which elusive death?

For Another Politburo Projected
(The Great Hall Convention)

Today, those bloated icons and brazen hacks will
Convene again here: squirrels in kinked fly whisks
Flushing their nausea will marvel at the cedar
Walls of The Great Hall gurgling their eulogies;
Hyenas with the guilt of our skulls behind them will
Tumble in chicken bones fattened by the meagre
Women of the village; brusque bumble-bees glutted
Will woo their dung-beetles – who will not show
Up here? We will all tune in to this levity, some
Plodding on to the dais, others shrugging without
Bitterness. And like yesterday, we'll forge no new
Vision, but nuzzling Adam and Queen Bee, we'll baa
The same anthem: when did our swastika ever starve?
– Unless some soldier-bee cracks in on us one day!

The 1984 Martyrs' Day Prayer

If this is how you'd have us pray to you, O Lord,
With this last egg from a matted bird startled
This scruffy coin from a street beggar beaten
This lean goat from flummoxed chaperons plucked

This sacrificial lamb from the shrines usurped
Our Chief's bull down their banquet halls flushed
Their abandoned adulteresses upon us 'rebels' set
This arena of schemers, scratching their boils in

Public, for another grave, unnecessary assault –
If this is how you'd have us praise you, O Lord,
Be gentle to this mortal, whose crime was only
The tipple on Martyrs' Day: break his neck nobly.

Chilling Jan Smuts Airport (In-Transito, 1984)

(For Lupenga Mphande)

I never thought I would reach this patch
Of carved Europe, landing thus cautiously;

I never imagined the musty air of this sudden
Limbo. How does one avoid racist metaphors

Where white dominates the shuffling morning
Queues ordering you into their passport slots?

(My Tanzania colleague insists no Boer stamp
In his passport!) Even those multiracial Air

Zimbabwe girls, charming in their confident
Shona, Ndebele and English a flight ago must

Mill around uneasy in the chill of Jan Smuts.
Elsewhere noisy kids would be sliding down

Those lovely escalators or running up and
Down trying to beat them; but here only giddy

White soldiers crowd the escalators though
No ANC threatens to molotov Jan Smuts Airport..

At the inquiry desk, the white woman in pink-
stuck smile immediately confirms the stand-by

Tickets from our white American acquaintances
With boarding passes best wishes to Manzini

And free access to Johannesburg delights but
She tosses us brown in-transito cards to get

Us into the lounge and buy us things though
The duty-free shop demands boarding passes before

Transaction: confessing our six hour stand-by
Also to Manzini, their transparent doors lock.

Our embarrassed Americans argue for our rights
But Jan Smuts' winking cues disarm such liberal

Efforts. And since your travellers' cheques are
Kindly cashed for you behind drawn bars, why don't

You join the other passengers in the lounge bar
Sipping beer, tea or coffee with chins-in-palms?

Watch that Zimbabwean white radical who's been
Through this before; she has been visiting her

Daughter married in Cape Town and now pours out
Her heart: 'When we reached this stage, sleeping

With guns under our pillows, we knew the war was
Over, but they do not understand in Cape Town

And I give then ten years!' she bets generously,
As fuddled, gasping glottals, cracking through

The microphones, marshal passengers to gate five;
She rises like a shebeen ghost staggering home –

Is it prudent to phone up Jaki at Skotaville?
I rake up Ingoapele's recent arrest in Soweto.

On Banning *Of Chameleons and Gods*
(June, 1985)

The fragrance of your banning order is not
Pungent enough after four years & one re-
print dear sister & your brother's threat,
Your chameleons 'poke at the raw wounds of
The nation!' won't rhyme however much you
Try – to ban, burn or to merely withdraw from
Public engagement, what's the difference? It
Still humiliates our readers, you & me. And
What do you see in these senile chameleons,
These gouty, mythical gods & libertine Mphunzi
Leopards to warrant all the heat? Haven't you
Heard the children's riddles yet or the jokes
At the market place about your chiefs & their
Concubines? How do you enjoy squinting only
At lines without bothering to ask what even
Swallows perched on the barbed wires of your
Central Prisons already know? Who does not
Know who pokes at whose nation's wounds raw?
& why should my poking at wounds matter more
Than your hacking at people's innocent necks?
No, for children's sake, unchain these truths,
Release the verse you've locked in our hearts!

April Wishes For 20 Gordon Square, London, (A Letter, 1987)

I

Dear Neil, as the toxic lizards of home crowd
In on us today, I remember those barriers in
Linguistics Gordon Square is so good at knocking
Down. You know how little I cared about those
Concrete gates that suspected me mugger on High
Street Barnet or framed in those hypocritical
Digs of Balham whether I sang about Wimbledon
Strawberries & cream or not. And knowing what
We know about dawns and bonfires, I believe I
Was not meant to map out Africa's dawn from
The dark alleys of London & I make no apologies
For being a late visionary. It was kind I was
Spared the Victorian euphoria of bowler hats,
Fly whisks & image fracturing London blitzes
That my fusty ancestors forever drill down our
Throats & flaked by those smoking tongues of
Brixton and Wood Green, it would have been
Dishonest to have pretended otherwise. So, here's
The season's peace for the crowd at the square!

II

And Dear Harun-Al Rashid, as the scorpions
Of Zomba gather at our keyholes to hear what
They have sewn, the kola nuts you offered me
Now sharpen. Jolting in that rusty, chattering
Citroen from the steel benches of Gordon Square
To the mouldy walls of York, I forgot to ask
Where you got kola nuts to break in the heart
Of London & the gates of York? And today, I
Discovered those photographs you forced on me

Boasting the York Linguistics Conference (with
Me sampling *Stones* and floating to inscrutable
Punk & you salaaming Mecca by the hour & steering
My 'rough' ways, you said). I hope you understand
Though: on my edge of Africa, without Opec Oil
Or golden stools to show off about, kola nuts
Were merely symbolic fetters, bitter, crumbly,
Not like spearmint gum & photographs cold.
But as the Shepherds Bush offals we shared &
The Daily *Mirror* cones we ate our chips from
Come back today, I thought you might like to
Look at these bristly negatives, with love?

The Seasoned Jacarandas Of Zomba

(For Frank Chipasula at Brown University, USA)

Stiff collared, hands in pockets,
Spitting out phlegm and scanning
The point of thankless patriotic
Wakes and timid nights, we lied
Brother, believing we would soon
Arrive, someone must hang around
To pick up the pieces knowing there
Would be no pieces, the true warmth
Was outside. Today, though seasoned,
Our metaphors blanch. The jacaranda
Still deeply purple our pavements;
But for once their pop under foot or
Tyre chills like the fresh squads firing –
Who'll watch whose wake tomorrow,
This self-imposed siege trembles!

The Streak-Tease At Mikuyu Prison, 25 Sept. 1987

(For Alec Pongweni)

It was not like the striptease at The Birds' Nest,
London Street, Paddington in the seventies, with

Each piece undone underscored by the thump of
Your pint of London Bitter & your analysis of

The structure of English pub vowels; nor was it
Like that male streaker, in the Three Day Week,

Stark & ugly, running around Talbot Square as we
Chuckled about the pleasures humans engage in;

The streak-tease at Mikuyu Prison is an affair
More sportive. First, the ceremony of handcuff

Disposal, with the warder's glib remarks about how
Modern handcuffs really dug in when you tried to

Fidget; then the instructions: take off your glasses,
Your sweater, your shirt, shove these with your

Jacket into their shrouded-white bag or your handbag
Until your release, which could be tomorrow, if you

Are lucky; and he seriously means release any day
(Haven't I heard about the four parliamentarians

Who stayed one night here, then got 'released'
The next day?) The spine chills at this revelation

& the prospect of another mysterious death; and if
Your naked belly should droop & you feel the stench

Of yester-booze, why blame God for abandoning you in
These walls named after figs? Now, the trousers' turn,

Strip by strip, to see the absence of razor-blades, pins
& pencils (these bring leg-irons & more handcuffs

Here). The pockets must be emptied of all other
Items too, especially 'the change' from Gymkhana

Club – nobody wants the reputation of stealing
Prisoners' change! And murderers awaiting hanging

At Mikuyu hide *chamba* & things in their anus, so
Do us the honour of bending. And the guards wonder

What pants University balls sit in, take that down
Too, though it's not yet law in Mikuyu to roll your

Banana (the humour is extravagant here). Finally,
The shoes & socks – pleading blisters on that bad

Foot brings another string of ministers & rebels
More distinguished, who have followed these rules.

Dare you fight further after ten hours in their cock-
roach custody? Let the shroud-white pocket-less

Gown & pocket-less shorts (they call them *foya*)
Wrap the shivering midnight body. Their questions

Are late, 'So, they took you from Gymkhana Club?'
Or their advice, 'You must be more careful, these

People are out to finish us, you see.' When locks
Give way, 'That Chemistry Professor friend of yours

Was the dullest I knew in Standard Six but now ...'
Now the stinking shit-bucket tripped over drowns

The news about the lights being left over night for
You to scare night creepers, as the putrid *bwezi*

Blanket-rag enters the single cell & staggers on to
The cracked cold cement floor of Mikuyu Prison.

Fears From Mikuyu Cells For Our Loves

Our neighbours' nerves behind those
Trimmed pine hedges of Chingwe's Hole
And the strategies they'll adopt when

They are approached by the Special
Branch are familiar but still horrify –
We rehearsed their betrayals weekly:

'Where did you first meet, I mean,
What did he often boast about in bars,
When he played darts, what jokes?

Did he, in your considered view,
Behave in a manner prejudicial? So,
He bent even the straight lectures!

Did your children ever mix with his
And how often did your wife share
Home-ground maize flour with his?'

We recycled other fears ad nauseam too
And what tricks to perform to thrive;
Only the victims' hour did we not know.

I remember, when our neighbour was
Taken eleven years ago, the secret tears
On my wife's cheeks, because visiting

His wife and kids or offering them
Our sweet potatoes in broad day was
A crime, her husband had just been

Invented 'rebel'; on the third day
University office quickly issued her
Exit visa to her husband's village!

The fears of our singular friends
We also reran: 'His detention was
Overdue, those poems! Don't mention

That name in my office; I hear he
Refused to apologise, how typical!
Why is that woman and her kids still

Occupying the University house?
Those conferences he loved, it's us
Going now. Has he reached Mikuyu then,

We thought it was another temporary joke!'
Today, I see your delicate laughter
And what abuse they'll hurl at you

Dear children, dear mother, my dear
Wife, as your 'rebel' dad confronts
The wagtail shit of Mikuyu Prison:

'Shore up their brittle feet, Lord!'

The Chattering Wagtails Of Mikuyu Prison

*(On transferring from the so-called VIP section of the
prison to cell D4 near the kitchen)*

I

Welcome to the chattering wagtails of
D4; before your Gymkhana Club story,
Let's begin with the history of the wing
You've come from. They call it the New
Building, which is so marvellously blank
As you saw, that you'd have cracked up
Within months, however tough-willed;
Thank these D4s for moving you here.

II

When the Secretary General of the Party
First conceived the New Building, it was
Done on behalf of the people, to liberate
Them from the despot they'd nominated
For life and who had extorted their
Traditional naivety to his craze. And
When the Chief of Special Branch chose
Himself head of detentions and detainees,
The two conspired to cure the monster's
Tics permanently here. So, they built
Those brown brick cells, four in front
And four behind, three paces by two
Each, white washing the walls inside,
To remind the tyrant of the bit of
Colour he would soon miss or to give
Him a chance to vent his wise yearning
In the manner of all graffiti. They
Separated the four front cells from
The four back cells with a thin wall

Through which you could shout messages
To each other at the risk of handcuffs
And leg-irons chained to the stocks.
They built a courtyard, sixty-five bricks
High, twelve paces long, four paces
Wide; an open flush-pit-latrine rested
In each courtyard to allow those most
'Trusted' henchpersons (including those
Brothers, sisters, nephews, nieces et al
And uncles of the official mistress)
To exercise their bowels after the coup
(A wobbly shower was bracketed nearby).
You saw that tough wire gauze knocked
Over the courtyard, it was to stop stray
Clods from the guards' kids outside falling
In and hurting the notorious dissidents
And rebels inside as they pined for the sun
In the yard. They called that adjunct
To Mikuyu Prison (where dangerous rebels
Like you first arrive) the New Building
Clearly as distraction from the horror
Imbedded in that infamous Dzeleka Prison
Where these squalid prison conditions
Were born, after our dear cabinet-crisis.

III

That annexe writ large, they'd christened
Mikuyu Prison where we circumcise you today;
And naming this prison after the noble
Biblical figs was flippant blasphemy to
Jesus who'd accused the figs of fruitless-
ness when he obviously saw it was out of
Season. But the Beast's remaining Party
Executives would have been gathered into
One of these eight large cells here, divided

90

Into fourteen little cells, two paces by one,
Named A-wing, where only grey-haired
Machipisa Munthali now clocks twenty –
four years (we call him the Nelson Mandela
Of Malawi, you'll recognise him by his
Shaven head every Christmas, in memory of
His mother, and the Chambers Dictionary he's
Allowed beside his Bible). In A-wing then
The Monster's ministers would reconsider
Their allegiances after the intended bloodless
Coup. And with the nation's doctors, teachers,
Diplomats, journalists, lawyers, pastors,
Farmers, and other nameless bumblebees,
Some seven hundred and eighty-eight freaks
Once (who'd have been released upon take –
over) cramming the other seven large Mikuyu
Cells, the pact would've been clinched
Without fuss. But didn't the Brute invoke his
Charms? The Chief of Special Branch and
The Secretary General of the Party crashed
Here, opening the gates of the New Building,
Mopping the wagtail shit of their creation!
The Chief eventually went bonkers and is
Quietly lodged at Zomba Central Prison
And the Secretary General opted to hang
(They had over-looked the cornerstone beacons
That attracted hundreds of wagtails outside,
Turning the wire gauze over the yard into
Overnight wagtail nests and shaping these
Nightmares that future detainees will mop!)

IV
We won't bother you with the cases of these
Sparrows in D4, talk to them to share
Their humour, but let not the years some

Swallows have clocked here horrify you
(Sixteen, eleven, seven, that's nothing!),
Rebels have been released here after one day.
Did you hear how `Dick Matenje, Aaron
Gadama, Twaibu Sangala, David Chiwanga
Got 'released' after one night at the New
Building and how the Special Branch who
Came to set them free suspiciously refused
To put their signatures in Gate Book 23
(Which carefully disappeared afterwards)?

V

But there's more. Take the other wagtails
Of Mikuyu Prison, these that chatter in
Circles, showing off their fluffy wings
To you, singing all day – watch how their
Splendour presages your visitors, if you
Are allowed any here; and do not scare away
These inmates, for, when acute malaria
Or cholera (we don't split these here!)
Admits you to Central Prison Sick Bay,
These wagtails will follow to minister
To you, these are the only priests allowed
Here, and the dragon-flies, the hundreds of
Moths in golden robes, the geese floating over
Us and more, bringing messages of cheer,
Foretelling releases to come. Don't laugh,
When the day locks up, these wagtails
Twitter another tale; you won't laugh
When this courtyard wire gauze fills with
Thousands of wagtails that sleep standing
On one leg, head under wings, snoring
About today, fabricating their stinking
Shit on the courtyard below for us to mop
Tomorrow; and everyday you must mop this

Courtyard to survive the stench; D4 has
Even devised wagtail shit-mopping rosters,
The very best in the land, definitely by far
Better than your skipping without ropes
At the New Building! D4 is divided into dawn
Shifts too, to ensure your choicest weevil –
infected red kidney beans from these pots;
Happily, D4'll spare you these dawn kitchen
Shifts, though the vampires of New Building,
Those ticks in the cracks of cement floors
Still testify here; and the fleas in the pores
Of your desert skin, those hyenas yapping
Worse than leprous midnight dogs, those
Scorpions whose sting sings like brain
Tumour, the swarming mosquitoes and bats –
What, who won't you find here, welcome
To the chattering wagtails of Mikuyu Prison

The Famished Stubborn Ravens Of Mikuyu

These could not be Noah's ravens, these crows
Of Mikuyu Prison, groaning on our roof-tops each
Day; wherever they wondered after their bungled
Pilgrimages in the aftermath of those timeless
Floods, Noah's ravens could not have landed
Here (they never returned to their master's ark).
These could not be Elijah's ravens either, for,
However stubbornly this nation might challenge
Lord Almighty's frogs, these devouring locusts,
The endless droughts and plagues, today, there's
No prophet God so loves as to want to rescue
(With the bread and meat from messenger ravens!)

These could only be from that heathen stock of
Famished crows and carrion vultures sent here
To peck at our insomnia and agony-blood-eyes
And to club the peace of this desert cell with
Their tough knocking beaks. And why don't they
Choose some other place and some other time?
Why must these crows happen at Mikuyu Prison
Always at dawn, hammering at the corrugated
Iron of this cell, drilling at the marrow of our
Fragile bones and picking at the fish-bones
Thieved from the dustbins we ditched outside?

Scrubbing The Furious Walls Of Mikuyu

Is this where they dump those rebels,
These haggard cells stinking of bucket
Shit and vomit and the acrid urine of
Yesteryears? Who would have thought I
Would be gazing at these dusty, cobweb
Ceilings of Mikuyu Prison, scrubbing
Briny walls and riddling out impetuous
Scratches of another dung-beetle locked
Up before me here? Violent human palms
Wounded these blood-bloated mosquitoes
And bugs (to survive), leaving these vicious
Red marks. Monstrous flying cockroaches
Crashed here. Up there the cobwebs trapped
Dead bumblebees. Where did black wasps
Get clay to build nests in this corner?

But here, scratches, insolent scratches!
I have marvelled at the rock paintings
Of Mphunzi Hills once but these grooves
And notches on the walls of Mikuyu Prison,
How furious, what barbarous squiggles!
How long did this anger languish without
Charge, without trial, without visit here, and
What justice committed? This is the moment
We dreaded; when we'd all descend into
The pit, alone, without a wife or a child –
Without mother; without paper or pencil
– Without a story (just three Bibles for
Ninety men), without charge without trial;
This is the moment I never needed to see.

Shall I scrub these brave squiggles out
Of human memory then or should I perhaps

Superimpose my own, less caustic; dare I
Overwrite this precious scrawl? Who'd
Have known I'd find another prey without
Charge, without trial (without bitterness)
In these otherwise blank walls of Mikuyu
Prison? No, I will throw my water and mop
Elsewhere. We have liquidated too many
Brave names out of the nation's memory.
I will not rub out another nor inscribe
My own, more ignoble, to consummate this
Moment of truth I have always feared!

To The Unknown Dutch Postcard-Sender (1988)

I

Your *Groeten uit Holland* postcard, with
Five pictures, dear unknown fighter for
My freedom, should not have arrived here
Really; first, your shameless address:
There are too many villages 'NEAR ZOMBA,
MALAWI', for anything to even stray into
Mikuyu Prison; then, I hear, with those
Bags upon bags of protest letters, papers,
Books, literary magazines, postcards,
Telexes, faxes and what not, received at
Central Sorting Office Limbe Post Office
Everyday, later dispatched to my Headmaster
And his henchpersons and the Special
Branch and their informers to burn, file
Or merely sneer at and drop in dustbins –
Your postcard had no business reaching
Mikuyu Prison. And how did you guess I
Would eventually sign my Detention Order
(No 264), October 21, and I desperately
Desired some other solidarity signature
To stand by (to give me courage and cheer)
However Dutch, however enigmatic, stamped
Roosendaal, posted Den Haag, 23 October
1988, to buttress this shattered spirit
And these mottled bare feet squelching
On this sodden life-sucking rough cement
Of Mikuyu Prison ground? But many thanks,
Many thanks on behalf of these D4s too!

II

You send me those Dutch tourist colours
I'd probably have spurned outside, but
In these soggy red-brick and cracking
Cement walls, a sun-burnt Dutch *clogger*
In black cap, blue shirt, orange apron,
Chocolate trousers and brown wooden shoes
Selling white, red, and yellow clogs,
Beside a basketful of more white clogs,
Is spectacle too tantalizing for these
Badly holed Levi's shoes and blistered
Feet! You offer me Dutch men folk in
White trousers and white shirts and red,
Blue and yellow hats declaring heaps on
Heaps of Edam cheeses on oval-shaped
Pine trays buoyantly shaming our ghoulish
Goulash of gangrenous cow bones mashed
In rabid weevil-ridden red kidney beans!
You proffer Dutch bell-shaped houses
Beside fruit trees, a family strolling along
The avenue – this concrete church with
Arches and Corinthian columns probably
Beat the bombs. A Dutch mother and daughter
In white folk-hats and black and white
Pretty frocks sitting on trimmed green
Lawn, offer each other red tulips beside
A colony of yellow tulips. And I present
You these malaria infested and graffiti
Bespattered walls, without doctors, priests
And twelve months of barred visits from
Wife, daughters, son, relatives, friends!

III

But, however these colours slipped through
Our post office sorters, your *Groeten uit Holland*
My dear, has sent waves of hope and reason

To hang-on to the fetish walls of these
Cold cells. Today, the midnight centipedes
Shriller than howling hyenas will dissolve;
We will not feel those rats nibbling at
The rotting cones of our toes. And that
Midnight piss from the blotched lizards
Won't stink; and if the scorpion stings
Again tonight, the stampede in D4 will jump
In jubilation of our *Groeten uit Halland!*

The Boxing Day Visit Of The Head Of Detainees

At the office gate, the guard-commander
Stands at attention. 'Special Branch!' he
Whispers, his forefinger crossing his lips.

The wooden bench creaks to my nerves.
I recognise the thin man. He ransacked
My life last September, scattering books,

Papers, records; violently quarrelling with
Mother and my six-year old, anger-choking
Son, 'You got cheek to bind my dad thus!'

He returned here in October 'for security
Reasons' to get me to sign my Detention
Order, 'Sign here, beside His Excellency

The Life President's own signature' (visibly
Photocopied from the Malawi Congress Party
Card of 1960s, perhaps for security reasons!).

The other man, double chinned, cheeks
Still puffed from yesterday's Christmas
Carlsbergs, has hands stinking of tomato-

boiled sun-dried fish he had for Christmas.
Why do they choose unlikely salamanders
To taunt us with death, further charges

Or freedom? Why don't they just minister
To their migraines at home after the hectic
Christmas chase of their vaporous rebels?

'You've been summoned to meet the Head of
Detainees.' I wonder what I'd be doing on
Boxing Day. 'I've been sent by Inspector

General to find out what your problems are.'
Silence. 'Have you got any problems then?'
Silence. Have I got problems? I can't talk

About the weevils in my food, I can't ask
For the medical doctor, not allowed here,
I can't want the priest, banned, I can't

Say, 'Even police magazine don't reach
Here!' I can't this, can't that, I can't –
'Yes, as a matter of fact, I do have two

Problems: one, I don't understand why
My wife and children are not allowed to
See me here; two, I want to apologise

But since I was neither charged nor tried,
How does one go about apologising?' Their
Eyes meet, gleaming. Head barks for paper

And pen. Guard-commander quickly brings
Five hundred ream of A4 paper and biro.
'If you put down here those complaints,

I'll take your letter to the Inspector
General personally myself, today. Take
Your time, we are here for you; we can

Wait for three hours, up to about one?'
The smell of fresh A4 paper overpowers,
The biro feels strange on fingers after

Fourteen months. I remember the tests I
Took in the dusty classrooms of Kadango.
After forty minutes and several drafts,

Humiliation resolves: you must apologise
About something, for somebody's sake, man!
Right: Dear Right Honourable Inspector

General, I do apologise, from the bottom
Of my heart, to His Excellency the Life
President, his government, his university

Authorities 'for any embarrassment caused
Or to be caused by my detention!' Also
As I left behind a very sick mother, wife,

Three asthma children, I do sincerely hope
Your Honourable Office can kindly get my
Case reconsidered. Your obedient servant...

The Head folds the two pages into his
Jacket pocket, assuring me the letter
Has arrived. The junior man touches me

Goodbye. The Head kindly offers to throw
My shredded drafts in the dustbins of his
Police Officers' Mess at home, I oblige.

The Tale Of A Dzeleka Prison Hard-Core Hero

(For Madhala)

'The Land Rover stops one hundred yards from
Dzeleka Prison gate; the two rows of those

Notorious guards you have heard about blur,
Their clubs or truncheons raised high to kill.

They unlock your leg-irons whose clump now
Numbs; they take off your handcuffs in blood.

Your garments are like Jesus's, except that
Like the other thief you have indeed robbed,

Many times, and several even armed. It was
The Congress Party wallet you threw in Shire

River that has brought you to Dzeleka Prison;
You could not stop pinching just to please

The name they gave this prison – how could
You stop picking the Congress Party mango?

It's the only fruit you pick without guilt:
They forced it off the poor, you off them,

Wash out! But you must run very fast between
The rows to get to the end of the human

Tunnel alive. I remember only the sudden
Naked shiver; the rest you can guess. Yet,

Imagine the whole Presidential tour to Taiwan
To import for us the one and only hard-core!

(Indeed, watch all those Western freedoms he
watched, wasted on such dull despotic desires –

The streets of Taiwani are so tidy, no thieves
No beggars – that's a nation for you! He boasts).

God, I miss those juicy avocado pears behind
The Congress Party fence in Kabula Old Museum!

And waiting to hang must be dead end here; I
Mean, there's no second chance in Mikuyu Prison

Is there? And that stupid traditional court
Judge, Moses, did he also ask you fellows to

Produce in court the person you'd sorted and
When you could not, did the devil also squeal:

Go and wait for your victim at Mikuyu Prison,
What village justice brought you to doom here?'

Tethered Border Fugitives Upon Release

(For Mercy & the children, 1991)

Upon release, when I was mad about those
Hasty grass-thatched mudhuts mushroomed

Below the grey boulders of Kirk Range
And the women & children who emerged

From them with the stench of civil wars
& harrowing tales (how senseless Mocambique

war-psychopaths *phanga*-skewered their
Sons' balls before their very eyes!), it was

Not their mudscapes (which reminded me
Of my childhood initiation grass-huts

& the dawn, ice-cold water into the ears
Poured by the harsh words of the village

Chaperons I'd escaped); it was the horror
Of those persistent mirrors I feared. And

When you wondered at those handshakes
Of American refined vegetable oils, those

Italian *carne bovina in brood* you bought
From the dear captives beside the tarred

Highway & brought into the shit-reeking
Cells of Mikuyu Prison 'to mend another

Dislodged mortal flinching in the muck
Of weevil-beans & the weeping bonfires

Of freckled geckos', you mocked; when you
Intensely succoured those border fugitives,

Did you expect to see this other ghost so
Tethered upon release wandering in exile?

The Straggling Mudhuts Of Kirk Range, 1991

(For T.S. Banda, Brown Mpinganjira & George Mtafu)

Four years ago, a battered initiate
Staggered out of those grass-huts
From a contraption of stunted weed,

Torn cartons and witch-oil-black
Cardboards held together by split
Bamboo and cords of bark; and trapped

In the heat between these hostile
Boulders and the misty valleys of
Villa Ulongwe, she nervously peered

Into the tarmac of our makeshift
Borders, her wind-blown babe suckling
At the bitter sweat of her dry breasts,

Her teeth (tartarred by wild fruits on
Flight) exposing embittered memories
Of yet another home charred, goats,

Ducks and chicks scattered by shrapnel
From the enemy: her own people. But
Today, from these sprawling mud-shacks

Permanently huddled below Kirk Range
And sometimes threatening to leap like
Sand-frogs in the rain but beaten back

Squatting, like those grey turtles stuck
Between Inkosi Gomani's dwindling grave
And the tarmac road; today, from this

Straggling shackscape a chaperon and
A boy defiantly declare their UNHCR
Wares beside the highway: tins of butter

From European Community Mountains,
Paraffin glass lanterns from Mozambique
And gallons of America cooking oil,

(Bartering for the much needed dry fish
The donors overlooked). Today, the mother
Even manages a bleak joke about her son's

Father 'who slunk back home to smuggle
What remained behind of his own but never
Came back!' But watch this woman tomorrow,

After the Berlin Wall, watch the trump
Card she mothers in this triangular struggle
For these rusty boulders. And she is

Not oblivion of the sand shifting under–
foot nor those *multipartisms* embarrassing
These starved implacable borders! Watch.

The Baobab Trees Of Nkope Hill

(For Nigel Wenban-Smith & John Craven, 1991)

In your multiparty promises, I fear
For those buxom baobabs most of
All, I fear he will invent other viral
Gimmicks to scupper those blossoming
Baobabs of Nkope Hill. He was never
Fond of exotic trees, you see, nor of
The children's riddles about them (God
Made me upside down, trunk without
Neck, fingers without palms, but food
And shelter, who am I?). He never felt
Close to such baobab riddles, let alone
The brightness of their ash-green hue.
You saw recently how melodies, mere
Melodies of one fish-eagle perched on
Baobab twigs, before swooping down for
His *chambo*, how mere voices threatened
Him!
                              Others
Dread the leeches of Milimbo lagoon,
Beside the lake, how they suck the thigh's
Blood as you catch little herrings on
Safety-pin hooks in dug-out canoes (and
You need fire to burn the stubborn buggers
Out!). But he has no quarrel with leeches,
Only the baobab trees, those lovely rows
Of baobabs punctuated by cactus (to keep
The elephants out). Will he allow more
Fish-eagles to sing on our baobabs then?
Won't he fudge another virus to smother
Those succulent baobabs of Nkope Hill?

Your Tears Still Burning At My Handcuffs, 1991

After that millet beer you brewed, mother,
(In case Kadango Mission made something
Of another lake-son for the village to strut

About!), and after that fury with the Special
Branch when I was brought home handcuffed –
'How dare you scatter this peaceful house?

What has my son done? Take me instead, you
Insensitive men!' you challenged their threat
To imprison you too as you did not *stop*

Your gibberish!' After that constant care,
Mother, I expected you to show me the rites
Of homing in of this political prisoner,

Perhaps with ground herbal roots dug by
Your hand and hoe, poured in some clay pot
Of warm water for me to suffuse, perhaps

With your usual wry smile about the herbs
You wish your mother had told you about.
Today, as I invent my own cleansing rites

At this return of another fugitive, without
Even dead roots to lean on, promise to bless
These lit candles I place on your head and

Your feet, accept these bended knees, this
Lone prayer offered among these tall unknown
Graveyard trees, this strange requiem mustered

From the tattered Catholic Choir of Dembo
Village. You gave up too early, mother, two
More months and I'd have told you the story

Of some Nchinji upstart who tamed a frog at
Mikuyu Prison, how he gave it liberty to invite
Fellow frogs to its wet niche, dearly feeding

Them insects and things but how one day,
After demon bruises, his petulant inmate
Threw boiling water at the niche, killing

Frog and visitor. And I hoped you'd gather
Some tale for me too, one better than your
Grand-daughter's about how you told her she

Would not find you on her return from school
That day. But we understand, after so many
Pointless sighs about your son's expected

Release, after the village ridicule of your
Rebellious breasts and sure fatigue of your
Fragile bones, your own minders, then your

Fear for us, when the release did finally come
You'd propose yet another exile without you –
We understand you had to go, to leave us space

To move. Though now, among the gentle friends
Of these Jorvik walls, I wonder why I still
Glare at your tears burning at my handcuffs.

Canadian Geese Flying Over Alison's House

(For Alison Gordon & Austin Clarke, July 1992)

When you wondered how Toronto summer
Rains could debase your barbecue before
That collage of artists and human rights
Sages reading at the Harbour Front and
Celebrating the identity of the African
Diaspora as you rescued your brazier,
Deftly separating the sizzling sausages
From glasses of sparkling 'Canadian' wine;

Do you remember my distracting you with
That splendour of Canadian geese flying
High above your house? I said, that chain
Of geese, flying thus over Mikuyu Prison
From Lake Chilwa toward Zomba mountain
Ranges, gently floating, criss-crossing, meant
The release of as many political prisoners
Within weeks (I counted eight flying over
Your house before Dany and I absconded
To Austin's post-mid-night mature rum!).

But when I returned to these lovely York –
shire moors and their peaceful Jorvik gates,
Did I have to wait for weeks to hear of
The last eight political prisoners I had
Left at Mikuyu Prison released (boasting
Nineteen, fourteen, ten, six ... four years
Of incarceration without trial or charge)?
I presume you are never bothered by such
Perhaps superstitious links, but I must confess
The lure of these and other liberation campaigns
Delayed my gratitude for your hospitality!

You Caught Me Slipping Off Your Shoulders Once

(For Tukula Sizala Sikweya Banda, 1992)

Today, when I heard of your release from Mikuyu
Prison after your fourteen years ordeal (for

Merely being nephew to your exiled rebel uncle
Or for winking at Inspector General's concubine)

I recall the frog you tamed (whose plot now
Thickens) and how you meticulously separated

The insects and craftily extracted the maggots
From those rotten cabbages in the dustbin heaps

Of Mikuyu Prison. I remember how your sharp
Breaths triumphantly bellowed weevils off those

Lobules of red kidney beans soaked overnight,
To salvage a semblance of a meal for us after

Moving me from isolation cell. You defiantly
Deflated the tedium of our years, cheering our

Despair with your contentious tales: you had
Smoked through worse horrors of Central Region

Mask dances (the birth place of this nation's
Brutality!), 'What lies here?' you challenged;

'And while I am Nyapala in D4, I will ensure
You outlive this poison ordeal!' you rasped

Venomously. Today, after outlasting all that
And in the comfort of these Roman walls, I

Hear those commands you shouted at me, often
At midnight as the hyenas howled, when you knew

I was awake, 'Come and watch this moon!' you'd
Whisper, 'It goes past that gap once a month!'

Sometimes at noon, Climb my shoulders, view
Those trees blossoming outside, you will be

Blinded gazing at these sick walls; climb these
Shoulders man, that beautiful woman with three

Children sitting under those acacias outside
(And brought by the priest in green car) could

Be yours; climb, damn it!' you would bark as
My nervous feet lept onto your lion shoulders.

I remember suspending tenaciously from the narrow
Window-sill and peeping outside in disbelief:

The green acacias dancing to Lake Chilwa breeze,
The chickens pecking under the guard's granary,

The jacaranda trees purpling in the distance,
The deep red flamboyant flowers, until my heart

Started, my feet began to sweat on your shoulders –
'My God, my wife and children! After twenty-two

Months! And Pat O'Malley in white collar!' You
Caught me mid-air, slipping off your shoulders

And mocking my timidity, watched the prison gates
Call my name. And today, from these peaceful

Jorvik gates, I gather, you and all those D4 wag-
tails can now see the whole moon? Amnesty!

The Souvenir Shards Of My Berlin Wall

(For Wilfried Ruprecht, Philip Spender, Peter Ripken et al, July 1992)

I

After our grave dialogues in Postsdam's Eduard-
Claudius-Club (about the things that fall
Apart or perceptions of our misconceptions!)
Between writers of what was Eastern Europe
And writers of what still is Africa (Diaspora
And all – the thought often mind boggles!),
After the warm reunions with long lost friends
And artists, some unknown but long admired,
After humbling presentations of signatures
In my book of poems and letters by writers
And linguists (from London, Edinburgh, Glasgow,
Kampala, Rotterdam, Dar., Vienna, Hamburg, Paris,
New York, Harare, Ibadan. Brussels, Kinshasa,
Berlin, Gaborone, Toronto, Soweto, Ife ….),
After the solidarity dockets of the struggle those
(Distinguished demonstrations, the festivals,
Awards, readings, verses, T-shirts, what not!)
For my liberation by mortals and mentors
Who adopted this prisoner of conscience –
Fear for this Mondialism now overwhelms!

II

Tobias Bange rightly questions the wisdom
Of my tears at this gathering and suggests
Instead, and perhaps characteristically, a TV
Interview within the walls of the Staats –
Sicherheit Ein Haus in Potsdam (that State
Security house in Potsdam that innocently
Mingled with trees, shops, offices and refused

To be named prison, for security reasons!)
To offer me the rare chance to see the arch
Brutality of German prisons once, in the light
Of my Mikuyu Prison, (the ironies never end!).
I accept and re-examine yard-and-cell whose
Sick dimensions are now peculiar classrooms!
Tobias Bange tempts me with the shattered Berlin
Wall and Brandenburger Gate to walk through
(However late in the day for me). He takes
Shots and buys me shards of the Berlin Wall
In plastic souvenirs sold by ex-Communist
Soldiers. I brood over the new walls European
Verse is bound to invent and what strategies
Capitalism will adopt to survive or repair
Centuries of totalitarian onslaught! Pause.

III

We stop on Niederkirchner St between two
Walls where metres of the original Berlin
Wall still stand tattooed in huge indelible
Graffiti – TACHELES! And fenced in tough wire –
gauze for future generations and me, flanked
By Gropius Museum on the left and another
Mock Berlin wall decked in colourful graffiti
On the right flanked by new scaffoldings
Of the ancient Prussian Parliament building.
Between these two walls (where Gestapos
On shifts jumped off running trucks once,
To shoot climbers to freedom), there's drama:
A Woman pulls out a hammer from her hand –
bag and begins frantically knocking down
The fake wall to bemused family tourists
(Who won't tell the clods of the true Berlin
Wall from crumbs of the fake Berlin Wall!)
Within minutes those once much dreaded

Polizei are on the scene. But this can only
Be another minor misconception best
Resolved with bows and smiles all round
These fragile times of transition to sanity –
Tobias Bange blames it on the Berlin heat,
'Soon we'll be eating our own bananas!'

IV

It's now that I recall your office Wilfried
Ruprecht, I hear you defying the sun-burnt
Gardens of our cardboard Capital Hill (where
Marauding hyenas prowl within stubborn walls);
I remember how you gleefully recounted
The paradoxes of your Berlin Wall which
Miraculously crumbled while I was chained
And how nobly you took the indignity you
Suffered for our redemption at the hands of
Our stony ghosts. I beamed, imbibing Nelson
Mandela's release in disbelief and contra –
distinction to my own, mean and weeks old,
Pondering your multipartisms, human rights,
Good governance etc., fearing the traumas
These would open up amongst our impervious
Ravens and the stench of their dungeon
Bats. You thought I was too civil with
My summation of your unique face in this
Curious strife for Africa's new dependence;
For, I saw the diffuse shapes future brushes
Would paint to your memory and was jealous;
But I warned only about our slipping grass –
roots and the impeding bloodbaths to be
Invented by our turgid cockroaches; you
Sincerely hope the wounds wouldn't happen.

V

But today, as Tobias Bange points to more
Scaffoldings of apartments in Potsdam
And Berlin (where Politburo Executives
Still live in fear of their own images),
War-cries of home rebound, I see distant
Kitchen Revolts of students and workers
At Chirunga Estate and Matenje Village
Where rosaries are flying for new banners
Of familiar perceptions of our deceptions.
Thirty-three years ago Ndirande was locked
In the Clock Tower Riots that liberated us
From British claws, now after the Bishops'
Pastoral Letter, Ndirande township still spills
The blood of independence not yet achieved!
Tomorrow they will scatter Ndirande, I fear,
To punish those riotous township rosaries
(And the world will probably turn away
Tangled in the exigencies of their Sarajevo) –
I decipher the shard of my Berlin Wall.

For Madame Potiphar's Wasteaways

*(To the memory of Alick Kadango, Sylvester Phiri and Frackson
Zgambo who died mysteriously in Mikuyu Prison after my release)*

The tale of your sudden deaths invokes weird
Belly-aches of what might have been. I did not
Know you as protesting rebels who might meet
Their end tortured under the pretext of cerebral
Malaria. How could those dreams of motels
You madly designed and re-designed (with
Our stolen chloroquine tables) all over
The coarse cement floors of Mikuyu, how
Could that generous humour have gone to
Waste so? Today, the blue jokes you trusted
Me with (on the origins of your ordeal)
Flash past: yours was the folly of willing
Fugitives netted in Madame Potiphar's soap
Operas, you said, and however dearly Madame
Potiphar desired to bid in your private and other
Businesses, you were neither Josephs lodged
Permanently with Yahweh nor did you intend
To govern Egypt's precious gold: yours was
The dull crime of staunch bodyguard loyalty.

So, Madame Potiphar need not have bothered
To cast her eyes on your tunics, imputing
Fantasies she had already fulfilled. And why
Did she have to chuck you into dungeons
When she knew you had no power to interpret
Pharaoh's dreams to deliver yourselves? But
Perhaps you were too naïve, my dear brothers,
You know how our vultures devour their young
Boasting about the shame they've never had;
How did you let them invent malaria for you?

Whatever, though I made no pledges, today
I feel guilty; they should have granted you
Full view of those stars we fought over on
D1 spy-window; they should have freed you
Like all those inmates we left behind now
Freed and actively liberating their Mikuyu
Dreams from the claws of our stubborn vultures.

In Memoriam (For Orton Chirwa, Edinburgh Cathedral, 20 October, 1992)

I

'Did you ever meet him in prison? How
Was he? We hear he's in leg-irons and
Chains for having attempted to smuggle
Out a letter?' Orton Chirwa, it's months
Now since your anxious friends pestered
Me about your health, shuffling those
Letters you wrote them in the struggle for
The liberation of Nyasaland from British
Rule. We admired the tone you chose to
Beat the subtle understatements of Colonial
Office and wondered how that compatriot
You'd offered the colours of the Malawi
Congress Party you'd founded could have
Eventually chained you and your wife for
Life? Where could we have gone wrong?
Orton Chirwa, four years ago, I entered
At midnight, the single cell of the New
Building Wing of Mikuyu Prison they dumped
You once. The walls of what they called
The VIP section of the prison spoke loudly
Your fanatics' tattoos: *O.C., Q.C. was here, OK?*
And though you had moved when I arrived,
The legend of the foya-gowns you stitched
Together to make a mimicry of bed sheets,
To supplement your Chiperoni blanket rags
(Which probably wrung your neck today),
Your lore continued to urge us to combat
The stench of Mikuyu bats without bitterness.

II

But when they consigned you to those walls
Of Zomba we secretly feared for your brittle
Constitution. How were those rheumatic
Bones going to cope in another lonelier
And darker cell of Zomba Central Prison
Beside the executioner's tools? How would
You get bulletins to bench your humour
On, and at what price, what leg-irons,
What handcuffs, what numbing chill of
Buckets of cold water on your naked body
For three days without food or water – what
Pneumonia we loathed! And today, I hear
They have frozen your fighting spirit
In the cramped mortuary of Zomba General
Hospital; will nobody mourn the rebel?
Will your dear wife (who probably took
Days to hear of your death) be allowed
To your burial? What of those children
With whom you shed tears in prayer for
Our country's independence, will they
Be allowed to travel to mourn their dad?
Will that Livingstonia Presbyterian Choir
Sing your favourite psalm twenty-three?
And will they bury you among your own
Or in that cemetery near St Mary's where
They bury nameless, nondescript people?
(Whatever, may you rest in peace, for tomorrow,
From the chaos of our democratic fronts,
A monolith will tower to your memory and
The memory of those heroes and heroines
Our country may try to erase, peace, peace!)

From
Skipping Without Ropes (1998)

The Following Dawn The Boots

The following dawn
I woke up to the reality of prison
Boots, jangling keys and streaks of the golden sun
My bones, muscles and joints –
My whole new plight stiff.

'The most dangerous rebels start out here
They may then be moved to other minor prisons
Or perhaps promoted to the general cells inside;
Even that 'legendary gang of four' came here first
At dusk, after lock-up; I commanded my guards
To chain them to the stocks in the cell you slept last night
(You have never heard notables
Crying like naughty children!)
The next day the rebels were released
Although the Special Branch who liberated them
Refused to inscribe their names and signatures
In Mikuyu Prison Gate Books
As they had done when they brought in the prisoners
That's when we saw something suspicious
About their kind of liberation;
So when we heard radio announcements
About their intention to cross the border at Mwanza
And their supposed accident there
The guards on duty hastened to bear witness
To the Mikuyu Gate Book inscriptions
Of the Special Branch who had freed their eminence –
But, truly, men have been reprieved within days here –
Welcome home!'

The guard commander had intended
The tale to chill me into submission
From the first day of my arrival

He wanted no hunger strikes
No jumping over prison fences
No protests, no nonsense in his prison,
He invoked my university mentors
The country's most 'notorious' rebels,
Demagogues and others who had felt
The sharp grip and blister of his Sheffield
Handcuffs, leg-irons, chains without blinking;
I embraced only his tale of the Gate Book engravings
Imagining someone found it mattered some day.

Skipping Without Ropes

I will, I will skip without your rope
Since you say I should not, I cannot
Borrow your son's skipping rope to
Exercise my limbs; I will skip without

Your rope as you say, even the lace
I want will hang my neck until I die;
I will create my own rope, my own
Hope and skip without your rope as

You insist I do not require to stretch
My limbs fixed by these fevers of your
Reeking sweat and your prison walls;
I will, will skip with my forged hope;

Watch, watch me skip without your
Rope; watch me skip with my hope –
A-one, a-two, a-three, a-four, a-five
I will, a-seven, I do, will skip, a-ten,

Eleven, I will skip without, will skip
Within and skip I do without your
Rope but with my hope; and I will,
Will always skip you dull, will skip

Your silly rules, skip your filthy walls,
Your weevil pigeon peas, skip your
Scorpions, skip your Excellency Life
Glory. I do, you don't, I can, you can't,

I will, you won't, I see, you don't, I
Sweat, you don't, I will, will wipe my
Gluey brow then wipe you at a stroke
I will, will wipe your horrid, stinking,

Vulgar prison rules, will wipe you all
Then hop about, hop about my cell, my
Home, the mountains, my globe as your
Sparrow hops about your prison yard

Without your hope, without your rope,
I swear, I will skip without your rope, I
Declare, I will have you take me to your
Showers to bathe me where I can resist

This singing child you want to shape me,
I'll fight your rope, your rules, your hope
As your sparrow does under your super-
vision! Guards! Take us for a shower!

Season's Greetings For Celia (BC)

They say when God closes one door
He opens a window to let in the sun,

Celia, your season's greetings arrived
In time of despair, after I had signed

My life out by signing the Detention
Order insisted upon by my Life President,

Who wants us to rot, rot, rot forever
In this prison, but your white and red

Roses invoke that 'War of the Roses' I
Battled to comprehend to achieve my

A-levels; the green English landscape
Summons the Romantics I explored

Under the billowing smoke of paraffin
Tin-can lamps once upon the tough terrain

I thought I had left behind; and how did
You hope to be remembered when you

Mark your name merely as Celia (BC)?
If the parantheticals are the British Council,

10 Spring Gardens, London, I recall no one
By that name there; my British Council

Programme organiser with whom I shared
My *London Magazine* poems was called

Sheila, I think, and why, why of all those
Bags and bags of protest mail which harass

The Post Office Sorting Centre everyday,
As oblique couriers convey, why did only

Your postcard from London and another
From The Hague choose to slip past our

Strict mail sorters at this crucial moment,
What bribe did you provide the Office-in-

Charge of prison for him to chance me to
His office to peruse your mail from over –

seas, defying the edict from the life-despot
And risking his life and mine? No matter.

Your season's greetings Celia have thawed
Our anguish furnishing these rancid prison

Walls with much sought after night jasmine;
Now the cliché glowers: somewhere some –

one we do not know cares – and that dear
Celia is all the prisoner needs to know!

Our Doctor Mr Ligomeka (In Memoriam)

I do not know why you return today
Shouting at Mikuyu Prison guards that
You wish to detect the effect of *fansidar* your
WHO brand of malaria tablets on your patients,
'Open the gates for Mapanje!'
When the timid prison guards bring
Me to your Sick Bay you demand privacy
'So I can have a proper look at his abscess!'
And as they reluctantly retire we have a soft laugh –
How nervously the idiots accept doctors' orders!

But you have come to tell me the story of my death,
You clarify, 'The nurses at the General are grieving
Your death which some authority has devised,
I came to verify for myself; now that I know, I
Will march you to the full view of the General!'
How you plan to perform this feat bemuses
But the message is clear,
When another bout of malaria strikes
I must not be excited about
The new brands of quinine the prison offers –
They could be poisons.

Besides, Martin Kanyuka, student, colleague, brother,
Has just been accidentalised,
'What I detest most is why they refused to let
Me do the post-mortem when they said it was
Just another accident!'
When you name three other university friends
Accidentalised in my short absence
My voice falters fearing,
'Won't you too vanish if they discover
The tricks you perform for us in prison?'

My dear doctor, you came to serve us
After inveterate wars for our medical liberation,
Our appeals had flown to the freedom lovers
Of the globe, through friends, dedicated strangers
And official bags before you were offered to us;
The weeping blisters and thick boils you exploded
On our groins and between our buttocks
Could not have been for nothing,
How could we have dreamt them up
On buttocks already inured beyond baboons?

Do you recall the bones that clinked
Squatting before you and the eyes
Deep in drooping sockets pleading
For your prescription of valiums
To manage Mikuyu's sleepless nights?
And those smelly lumps of *nsima* you
Extracted from cheJumo's ears were
No mean madness, cheJumo frankly
Sought to protect his ears from the tyrant's
Tedious tales that had damned him here!

So, when we hear you too have been
Accidentalised today, we are not surprised
But pray that wherever you are you might
Still shelter the patients of the Sick Bay
You have left behind.

Hector's Slapping Of Mama's Brother
(Or When The Second Release Left Us Behind)

I

Amnesty came like a whirlwind gathering
The courtyard's brown leaves, bird feathers,
Blanket threads, dust, tossing them about,
Twirling them through arid water drainages
To the world outside. Hector and the others
Were gone! Today, with the marabous un-
caged, leaving the present aching oversights
And chasms for the black-wing stilts to wade
Through the swamps of the vast marshland
They have left us behind, and to scour this frog
Roe as the mosquitoes wail on their lily basins
Around the wash, now that Hector and more
Than twenty marabous have been liberated
Leaving us alone, unwanted, sterile, I dread
The time our turn will come, shall we sing
Those praises to God throughout the night as
The marabous temporarily held in the New
Building Wing of the prison did before being
Let loose, shall we smile at one another freed
After those wars we have endured over food,
Medicines, freedom, gods, these many years?

II

Hector's last battle over my valiums was bitter,
'I have no more valiums left,' I try to explain,
'Use your influence then!' Hector barks back,
I ran into my cell to cry the hurt to sleep; when
I hear Hector's war with another mate erupting
Mainly frustrated by my valiums, the guards

Assault the courtyard truncheoned for murder
Only to detach the bleeding adversaries then
Lock them up in punishment cells chained to
The stocks, handcuffed, leg-ironed and naked;
No water, no food, three buckets of cold water
Poured onto their frigid bodies, then felled on
The cold cement floor to swim for three days.
Today, I still hear Hector's comrade in his cell
Shrieking, remembering his mother. The war
Had begun with Hector boasting, only he was
The Man in Mikuyu for plucking the temper
To bruise life-despot's concubine's brother in
A brawl; Hector had claimed Mama's brother
Had breached their New Bakery's overtime
Intruding into their shifts and insisting on their
Adulation of his management of the bakery
The 'royal family' had snuffled; he had argued
His comrade had only drunk himself to shit!

III

Today, those marabous are gone, actually set free,
Leaving us to recall the order the cell suffered to
Dossier Hector's battle for the Officer-in-Charge or
Else; I hear one proposition from the corner cockle,
'We must swear the war was over breadcrumbs
Which inmates on Special Diet had offered both
Combatants, their scramble for breadcrumbs has
Turned this nasty – that way O.C. will comprehend
Why we all need Special Diet!' Peals of laughter;
Another proposal ensures: let's offer the fighters'
Tribal colours as cause, thus nettling life-despot's
Dictate on 'contact and dialogue' already crumbling.
'No!' issues from the corner, 'Let's tell the truth:
Marabou Hector was being frog-puffy to presume
Only he could have staked the slapping of Mama's

Loathed brother, nobody could stand the boast.' I
Remember us finally resolving that the battle was
Not to be about my valiums lest the O.C. banned
Those too; that night I recall sitting on my empty
Toilet, picking a pencil lead piece from my kinked
Hair, scratching my toilet paper for *more valiums*!

When Release Began Like A Biblical Parable

When the prison gates opened for apostle Simon
Peter who was sleeping, chained-double, guarded
By four squads of four Roman soldiers each, when
The angel's blinding flash tapped his quiescent side
The decisive chains on his blistered wrists suddenly
Dropping, when he belted up, the soundless sandals
Springing as he gathered his cloak around him on his
Way out, why, why did Peter not believe the vision
Until the last solid bar gave way on the Lord's own
Terms, the angel abandoning him unfettered outside,
Alone, as The Rock, liberated from Herod's clutches
Returned to his praying Antioch Church, stunned?

And why should this firefly at the back of another Land
Rover whose bleached canvas stutters in the whining
Wind speeding nowhere believe, why must I believe
Minded by these nervous guards as my Special Branch
Driver ravages his boiled groundnuts without a wink;
Why should my crumb of Lifebuoy, my toothbrush with-
out its teeth, my toothpaste flattened clean, this partiner
Of holed Levi's shoes, this polythene kilo of sugar (for
Porridge wherever I am going, said the Officer-in-Charge),
Can this be the reprieve of this flustered Peter the clod –
Your late disciple, Lord, without the stuff to lean on?
Let the dazzling dust of distant familiar mountains,

Let these eternally dry maize fields, the truncated leaf-
less mango trees that feel taller than blue gums (Your
'Ephpheta', Lord, brings such clash of memories I did
Not dream I would ever see again!), let peculiar colours
Soak up then, let the Land Rover's rails rattle as I blink
At my Officer-in-Charge: We do not know what it is,
As you know, nobody tells us anything but if it's transfer

138

To another prison, take your sugar, if further questioning
Further charges, we'll welcome you back, if release, best
Wishes, remember the friends you leave behind, other-
wise, we'll note the Gate Book names of your assailants
For your wife and children or for posterity, good luck!

Our Friend Inspector General
MacWilliam Lunguzi

I

Forty-three months ago he frolicked as
Chief of Special Branch, boasting infinite
Access to the ubiquitous face on the walls
Of the country wards, 'I report directly
To him!' he pointed at the despot's image
On his office wall; forty-three months today,
He gloated over being Catholic too though
Slipped, could fellow Catholics trust each
Other then with the truth nothing but what
Might have riled the Life President to direct
His officers to arrest and detain? 'Tell me
Who reported you directly to HE, I myself
Will implore the Life President's clemency!'
When I offered my forehead wrinkles for
My repentance, he taunted me with, 'You
Must pray three Hail Marys of your rosary
For His Eminence to forgive and review
Your Friday 25 September, 1987, detention.'

II

But today, after his three Hail Marys have
Become my stinking three and a half years
And his promotion to Inspector General
Of the country's police, we have met again
He anxious to please, me suspicious about
This brusque invitation to his catholic office –
His antique scroll of stubborn tales unlocks:
He has been trying to change the monster's
Spots since we last spoke, 'Glance at this
January memo to HE,' he retorts, 'What
Does the margin of my memo to him say?'

I see five names, with 'Approved' in black
Ink against the first four, 'Never', against
The fifth, mine, inscribed by His Excellency's
Initials which he always dated. 'My friend,
You were prisoner never to be freed in those
January and February releases you missed.

III

'But today, I flashed another card, Presidents
In other countries free political prisoners on
Their official birthdays, on HE's next week,
Why doesn't HE in his wisdom reconsider
Our story of those political prisoners who in
Our view have repented and will be under
Your Excellency's trusted police surveillance
Anyway, though I hate to bring this list of only
One political prisoner, Your Excellency, Sir!'
He fishes out his latest memo to HE for my
Tears to bear my name capped in the middle
Of his memo. 'Do you see what's on the margin
Of my May memo to His Excellency?' When
I read 'Approved' , see Life President's dated
Initials my heart sinks, my eyes boggle as he
Points at HE's portrait on the wall and declares,
'HE is pleased to have you released, return to
Your wife and children before HE reshuffles
His cards; note, at this point only three people
Know you're being released, HE, myself, yourself!'
As his words begin to mean, my unshackled
Feet linger, pondering 10 May 1991, outside!

Tamya's Shepherd's Pie, 10 May 1991

Child, this shepherd's pie you offer this starved
Stomach this late Friday afternoon, this china and

Stainless knife and fork you place in his hands, this
Glass of orange, your civil genuflection, your voice

So delicate and your wonder at the return of another
Denuded memory witnessing the purple jacarandas

Strewn on the rocks and avenues of Zomba plateau –
My dear child, do not ask where this bundle of blunt

Tissue before you comes from and where it proceeds.
Having left behind other unsullied souls fumbling for

Breath and gnashing clods of rubbery weevil-ridden
Pigeon peas from crumpled enamel mugs and maggot-

ridden maize *nsima* on holed rusty plates; besides,
Denied the luxury of cutlery in those flaming beacons

Of prison visible at night from where you stand, this
Bundle of memories is not your Peter knocking on his

Disciples' Church door nor Lazarus resurrected, this is
Your Mulungusi Avenue rebel uncle returning from

That eternal abomination to which they slung him –
'Could I give your auntie the fright of a lifetime call?'

The Risen Lazarus At Very Tedious Last!

I used to wonder about the details of the risen Lazarus,
Not merely how thankful he must have been to Jesus for
Raising him from the dungeon of death after four days
Nor the unbelieving bystanders, startled then stupefied,
But how Lazarus managed to get up with his hands and feet
So tightly strapped by ribbons of death, his face blinkered
Like a hostage; how he must have bashfully wriggled as
They sheared the shroud after Jesus had intoned, 'Untie him'.
I dreaded his rotting body too, once catacombed always …
Even Sister Mary conceded, 'Lord, four days, the stench!'
And does the tomb stench just disappear at resurrection?
What welcome tears run down their cheeks, what embrace?
And were Martha's hot porridge and Mary's warm bath
Water sprinkled with crushed herbal roots and leaves to
Sever Lazarus from the dead as we do when the prisoner
Is released from Mikuyu, say, after three and a half years?

What bothered me above all, and I fear bothered Lazarus
As well, was the global truth that there would be no second
Time, once Lazarus died again, after Jesus Christ had really
Gone, there would be no second time for Lazarus to return
To his beloved sisters until perhaps the very final day. So,
Now that this Lazarus is home and dry, the stars inmates
Scrambled over in our Mikuyu Prison cells are for grabs,
This Lazarus must watch every assembly, ritual and feast
Of the Sanhedrin for those further charges the Officer-in –
Charge noted at send-off; those mates Lazarus once knew,
The company he cherished, the bottle particularly – he will
Have to ruefully bolt; and though it's fear of the everlasting
Pit that baffled Lazarus, it must have calmed his nerves
To feel again that dusty clay of home at very tedious last!

The Sinful Scribe Of Kabula Hill, Blantyre

I

You recognised her by the way she was
Slipped into your office by the despot's
Drivers and messengers without fanfare;
You inspected the name that was meant
To be your secretary (weren't you at her
Interview and appointment?) Today,
You saw another face that did not match
The qualifications you had anticipated;
This was recommended by the highest
Authority, 'Came from above,' you were
Told. You dared to invent a fib, 'Which
Malawi Young Pioneer Paramilitary Base
Did you indicate you had got your driving
Licence from, as I recall your application
Forms?' Often you needed no loaded lies
But only charged her to type your memo
To the censors on *Animal Farm* banned.

II

Today, after your three years and seven
Months in detention, she dashes after you
Anxious to tell her story; she swears by
Her ancestors all she knew was typing,
She did not do what the other secretaries
Were famed to do; now she just wanted
To say she'd been bothered by the letters
She typed for her master, your colleague
Once, elucidating your verse to the higher
Authorities when they still kept you inside;
This thing's been chewing at her heart these

Years – the poor scribe forever had a heart!
Now that you are unchained, she thought
She might snatch this opportunity to recount
Her tale, but she must catch her bus, 'Thank
You for your attention.' Wait, you interrupt,
Blessing! Absolution! Lord, is she gone! You
Open the confessional for the next sinner.

Another Clan Of Road Fated Shrews

No, they have not gone, the cockroaches that
Snuffed the radiant hue of our calabashes
And crashed on the walls of our prison cells
Where their shadows tracked us down; we
Were foolish to assume they would retreat
Into the crevices of their pallid orders those
Vipers now changing their skins shameless;
We should not have anticipated their nerves
Screeching and springing from branch to branch –
Watch them darkly even! Must we therefore
Cede to another dance whistling yet old tunes
Like we have not been circumcised harshly,
Must we surrender to the sallow faces which
Consigned these brittle bones to the reeking
Pit we happily left behind? Do I dare to linger?

No Mother

Excuse this arrogant spectacle but with such
Furrows of tears on your daughter's breast
And the children's nimble cheeks, I will not
Chameleon colour another life. Why must I
Who've suffered everything, conceding none,
Inflict on your daughter, these children, more
Weeping verrucas from the cockroaches that
Have sucked their feet for slaying nobody? I
Will travel, however briefly, however painfully,
I will assemble drier twigs from distant ravines
For the fishermen's bonfire of another dawn.
I will venture far away where navels of alien
Hounds inspire mothers to conceive squirrels
And not the road fated shrews that we are!

The Vipers Who Minute Our Twitches

'Son, venture into distant rolling terrain
And marvel at God's umbilical cordage
Of peculiar hounds!' Uncle, this abrupt
Liberation, this dogged fear for our safety
From friend or foe, is cause enough; may

These wavering village voices, therefore,
These distressed handshakes of relatives
Who tremble to see us off, hurt; when did
Our political dissenters ever procure proper
Goodbyes from their dearest ones here?

So, let the families of your kinsfolk dear,
Let these nephews and cousins mustered
In defiant solidarity make their hurried
Backhanded hugs before the informers
Gathered about register who was present

At the rebels' send-off, though what galls
Us now, if we are truly free, is whether ours
Are the last feet to abondon this beloved
Territory in disgrace, for having lynched no
One – is this the ban we so dearly dreaded?

May our expatriate defender in light T-shirt
Shrewdly extend his welcome wink then,
May he walkie-talkie our delayed arrival
To his compeer upstairs, we'll feign smiles
In wonder, irritation and beholden shame!

And yet what spectacle, my dear country,
What affront, what treason deserves this
Protection from you by kinder friends from
Far away? When did your warm heart go
Cold? And should we perhaps shake this

Tenacious dust off our blistered feet against
This beloved soil? What crime merits such
Covert parting on exit visas, exit air tickets?
And these children, these buoyant children,
Where will they get anchor to repair and ride

The battering swells of their foreign confines?
And this resilient wife, this house of gentle
Friends, what breach have these committed?
Uncle, which airport are we bound for, what
Story shall we claim we have landed to tell,

Which navels of alien hounds are we meant
To wonder at with our stubborn brood of folks
Left behind? And how long, Lord, will the vipers
Minute every twitch, laughter and tone of voice
Made by those sending off this rebel family?

The Delights Of Moving House, Tang Hall, York

When we first arrived in Tang Hall
The children welcomed us by stealing
Glances at us, sniggering over the hedge,
Milling about the front door hedge after school,
Spitting loudly, monkey-faking without ambiguity
Until some started throwing eggs at our windows,
Sometimes writing 'FUCK OFF' on the windscreen
Of the car we had bought near the scrap-yard.

Judy's laughter fired:
'How dare crowds of Tang Hall kids do this to chaps
Just rescued from the jaws of African crocodiles?'
Lunda joked:
'I wish they gave us the eggs they waste on our walls!'
Lika merely sulked as he mended his bicycle;
Mercy frenetically mopped the kitchen floor
Shouting, 'Hold on, children, what lies here?'
And I thumped my chest recalling my Latin
'Mea culpa, mea culpa, mea maxima culpa!'
I have sinned, I have sinned, I have sinned most grievously.

St Margaret Clitherow Of York

As the Yorkshire fox of this leafy autumn howls
Your rebel spirit Mrs Margaret Clitherow
Mocks the wondrous asylum my African
Village wisdom warned about:
In far-out lands expect to find
Hounds with weird navels.
Mrs Clitherow, the breach for which
York Sheriffs and Bailiffs gaoled you in York Castle
Then in Kidcote-by-Ouse-Bridge crushed
Four hundred years on, your saga unnerves;

Why do tyrants forever unleash provocateurs
To ensnare harmless recusants? Why did
York Sheriffs seek to yoke your contest
For the rights of minor Catholics seized
By the Elizabethan connoisseurs of death
When they knew you would never
Revoke your care for minority?

And when you watched, through your window,
Between the Shambles and the Pavement
Beside the Church of Holy Cross,
When you saw the city's executioners erecting
Scaffoldings to hang your mentor Thomas Percy
That 'dear of the whole people'
That true Earl of Northumberland
Whom you beheld writhing to his
Death – to the city's cheering street crowds
Who relished the executioner's drama,
When Judge Clinch 'legally' searched
Your heart for whatever he had sown
And prayed for you to be conformable
To his monarch's church after the travail

He fancied over his execution of pregnant
Rebel women; when the executioners
Quelled your bones *peine forte er dure*
After covering your groin with the habit
You'd embroidered for your own death;

Mrs Margaret Clitherow,
It was not just another
'Traitor by the holy blunder of papal bull'
They stilled for felony of harbouring priests
And sharing their bunker masses,
It was not a mere woman
Tending offal-and-tripe in her husband's butchery
That the judges interrupted,
It was more than your surreptious
Voice they smothered,
It was a saint!

And how could the courts not think
That six weeks after secretly burying you
In an obscure filthy city corner
Your ghostly father and cohorts would
Re-inter, Gregorian chant, incense and all,
Your 'Incorrupt body without any ill smell!',
Why did the rock that tore your skin
Piercing your heart,
That eight hundred bulk which
Splintered your tender ribs
On York's Toll-Booth-by-Ouse Bridge,
Why did they all conspire without seeing
That the vestige of your hand at the Bar Convent
And the lock of hair elsewhere
Would forever jeer their act,
Why were they not ashamed
Of the memory of the anniversary
When we would hallow your blood?

Saint Margaret Clitherow
As the bed-rock blasts the veins your
'Jesu, Jesu, Jesu, have mercy on me'
Still echoes; and in the other
Kingdom remember to pray
For these blind mirrors of your
Ecclesiastical arraignments
For whom you resurrect today
And will rise every October!

Another Guide To Clifford's Tower, York

When Border TV crew suggests that I try to annul
Some horrors of Clifford's Tower through Africa's
Peculiar prison lenses, the Tower's guide protests.
How daft! But I refuse to condemn lest the cracker
Has recycled so many terrors for other callers that
Our Border TV cameras perhaps scare his received
Creed about Clifford's Tower. And indeed, today,
Eight hundred years on, the city still tends Clifford's
Tower in golden daffodils which bloom throughout
The Yorkshire spring, and when Guy Fawkes comes
Round each year, you must gather beside the Tower
In balaclavas and winter coats to worship the local
Hero, watching your children watching fireworks
Fabricating rainbows in the dark sky but as you rub
Your tingling hands against Yorkshire's freezing
Breeze, do not weep with the willows of River Ouse,
Let the willows' dreadlocks hang loose like the sausage
Tree fruit you left by the River Shire many mountain
Ranges away; consider, rather, these to be the navels
Of those eccentric hounds of exile that your fathers
Warned about; your reward is the cool beer beside
The warm gas fire later; and remember to shout with
The children as their flaming Guy Fawkes shatters;
And forget Roger Clifford the Lancastrian rebel they
Harshly hanged after the Battle of Boroughbridge
Naming the Tower after him; forget the Sheriffs and
Bailiffs who summoned one hundred and fifty Jews
To burn themselves to death at the Tower for spurning
Insolvent authority and refusing to quash their loans
After the English King and defender of Jews had gone
On Sabbatical in Burgundy; and if the story of those
Jews who first fomented the daffodils in thoughtful
Memory of their own dead moves you, riddle out
The wilful tone of your guide to Clifford's Tower!

Heartaches In Norwegian, Bergen*

(for Helgë Ronning, Micere Mugo, Chenjerai Hove & Emmanuel Ngara)

As the dregs of our prison begin to settle at the bottom
Of another calabash and the times start to focus, allow
Me to over-indulge Helge: my dear fellow, this week I
Laughed when I imagined you camouflaged as tourist
At the airport on entering my country with solidarity
Messages from friends at Zimbabwe International Book
Fair, the Association of Nigerian Authors and others
Tucked under your sleeve, refusing to declare; what cheer
Your 'bulletins' brought smuggled into our grey prison
Walls, what chatter inspired, we only wondered why
You did not wait for our reply, did you fear the border
Characters would sniff the writer, critic and diplomat?

And today I arrived in Stavanger, that tip of the world
Where your pine public houses hang from the cliffs as
Thrashing waves roar below, our umbrellas perpetually
Dripping; today I drank your Skol on tap too touched
By the Norwegian sagas of your struggle for our rescue
From our despot's crocodiles, and I visited the suburbia
Of Bergen as you insisted – the snow capping the knolls
Dazzled blind; we even skidded for Bergen Philharmonic
Orchestra, where the flutes wailed for the liberation of other
Souls trapped in the distant dungeons of another globe.

But that buoyant little theatre in the heart of Bergen and
Ariel Dorfman's tale told in your Norwegian so accessible,
That was another time in another territory; for the woman
Who struggled to free herself from her torturer, that wife
Forced to take on a midnight lodger (the lodger whose car
Had broken down on his way home and the husband had
Wanted to play his Samaritan), the woman was raped by

The prison superintendent turned her midnight lodger,
She was viciously violated in the jail she was freed from
Nor is her anguish idle, for, isn't the woman the icon for
The ruthlessly raided who are forever forced to reconcile!

*After watching the Norwegian version of Ariel Dorfoman's
'Death and the Maiden'*

The Parable Of My Renault 4 Driver, Stavanger

It's like the story of any driver
In my part of the fourth world

There's a knock on the door
He's heard I've purchased a fifth-hand Renault 4

The guy next door has just got his licence through him
He proudly displays the credential that's done the trick

The fellow must worry about anything he touches
But six months later, I get my own driving licence too

Then the real bargaining begins
Do I seriously want to see him begging at the market?

The best way to celebrate my first-attempt driving licence
Is to get him a job among my university friends or colleagues

He makes no effort to conceal the intended blackmail
He believes I have enough clout

I casually suggest the police station
We part company in rather inconsonant smiles

A year later, his vehicle is policing roadblocks
Our story is sealed in mutual grins

Until recently, exactly sixteen years later,
I am madly trying to send a message to England

From the post office of his rural district
Where they exiled my wife at their hospital

(To punish her from my sins –
She now enjoys feeding border fugitives

From Mozambique at the weekends particularly
Sharing with the malnourished fugitive babies

Her little food and those priceless vitamins
She often brought to my prison cells!)

On the phone I accentuate each point
With my now familiar chorus

'Yes, three years, seven months, sixteen days
I have been released unconditionally ...'

But a booming voice behind me jolts
My British Council telephone conversation

'You are the most dangerous man I've had to deal with!'
I duck, to confirm it's not another arrest

My Renault 4 driver's story then unfolds:
After the police, he went to the post office

Where he's had the enviable duty
Of sorting out all my 'protest' mail

'Bags upon bags arriving from the world each day –
Where on earth did you get these friends?'

He apologises to my wife
He could not even greet her when I was still in

For fear of recrimination;
'But those bags upon bags –

Some we sent to your headmaster
Some to the Special Branch

Others to the Secretary to the President and Cabinet
A few books and magazines

We managed to derail to your wife here.'
But he mustn't talk too much

He must be off, wishing us well.
Today, from another corner of the globe

When this Stavanger pub in Norway recounts
And Bergen Philharmonic Orchestra underscores

The extent of the war of my liberation
The parable of my Renault 4 drivers still meddles.

On His Vain Search For Roosendaal

(For Martin & Kate Banham, 1994)

In vain did your firefly cross the The Channel, hoping
To avoid the stinging fog of the vale of York, landing
Among the ancient windmills and the mute mazes
Of the dykes the Dutch forever reclaim from the sea;
In vain did your African firefly burrow among these
Vandyke brown leaves of autumn choking the criss –
cross of canals, cluttering the serpentine dykes; in vain
Did your firefly drift with the swans and ducks or float
On these purple-blue notes of waterlilies, bemused by
The leaping fat frogs of Leiden; in vain did the firefly
Watch the dexterous Dutch invent tropical weather and
Tropical gardens where they grow the delicious cherry
Tomatoes you loved to swallow whole once; in vain
Did your firefly comb these restaurants where sizzling
Biefstuk Mozart vies with *Tong Picasso*; in vain did your
Epic quest for his Roosendaal, that netherscape virginal
Valley of roses where weed and serpent slumber among
The radiant roses as your firefly gurgles from bitter herbal
Concoctions of the gourds of underworld hunchbacks
Who hold the key for opening the doors to our follies;
In vain did firefly hack through thorny plots of Dutch
Women shouting their tulip prices and brightly clad lads
Their Edam cheeses; in vain all that; for today firefly's
Feeble feet began to tire over Roosendaal's antiques of
Those squiggles of signature scratched on Den Haag's
Groeten uit Holland postcard he received in prison far
Away, which he came to these netherscapes to recover.
And last night the snow was heavy; the vista around 272
Boerhaaverlaan is as white as coconut fruit split open,
The pigeons are gathering outside the window, scraping,
Pecking at the heaps of snow and cooing as if to mock

Your firefly's wasted hunt for his Roosendaal; let your
Yorkshire dales spring then, however scornful the harsh
Echoes of home; fix it for this firefly to scrape the snow –
laden hedges of Yorkshire; as for his Roosendaal, there
Will be another autumn to hunt the Dutch briars!

Antwerp: Chronicle Of An 'Other' Imperial Child's Encounter

(For Martin & Connie Mooij)

I

Today, this little city voted the Cultural Capital of
Europe last year, radiates with world bards brought
Here to celebrate another night of poetry on the road.
But why don't we make the local cultural viewing
Rituals first, why don't we catch those exuberant
Brushes of Peter Paul Rubens as they shimmer in their
Lustre of antique leather on the walls with Rubens'
Self-portrait glinting through the Baroque furniture
(Wasn't it his Christ's 'Descent from the Cross' I
Saw many London student years ago?) No matter.
But what chairs, what 'Rubenshuis' cabinets craftily
Chiselled, with their edges perfected by Hercules whose
Sinews cuffed, battle the lion beside flying archangels
'... And these concrete images of heads on these walls
Are the philosophers Rubens and the Archduke read ...'

II

Yet, watch, gently the city's regal esteem and images of
Another perfectly buried childhood spontaneously surface
Among the merry minstrels wired into Antwerp's cheer-
fully restored theatre, is it to mock our person or our verse
On the road? Never mind. I served Mass beside Mulanje
Cedar altars once and after ensuring that their flaming
Easter candles did not touch the winged wooden cherubs
And seraphs, I knelt down, offered my *confiteor*, crossed
Myself and left, little expecting this encounter with other
Original altars in Antwerp; ah, how the ancient sculptors
Might have deftly carved their oak as Rubens held his

161

Luminous court brushes! But watch, Lord Macaulay's
Africa choking under her village schools, 'Name Europe's
Two largest harbours,' confused hands up, the chorus
Throws up its mechanical 'Rotterdam and Antwerp!'

III

Then envision subtle colonial Arithmetic on London
Once, foxed under mission fig trees those pristine villages
Ago, we marvelled as imperial choo-choo trains left their
London Euston Station at six for Liverpool Lime Street
Two hundred miles away; if the trains travelled fifty miles
An hour, what time would they arrive, all being equal?
Our answers splash down David Livingstone's cataracts,
Surfing past the baobab trees of our Kasisi Traditional
Authority, nibs spill out ink as bounteously as bee-eater
Droppings adorn our Bishop Mackenzie's grave stone!
Or take only the other month when Wakefield Prison
Nursery rhymes our prime encounter 'Here we go round
The Mulberry Bush, Mulberry Bush, Mulberry Bush …'
How jealously the prison officers guard this primeval
Bush of Yorkshire for other buried imperial children –
Isn't it remarkable how our vulgar imperial idols mellow
With time, sometimes towering, to tone us down!

Watching Berthe Flying Easter Balloon

(For Ludo & Berthe Pieters)

I

When Michiel decided to surprise his mother on
Her seventieth birthday at Easter, he had no idea
How it would go. 'Let's give her a treat of her
Lifetime, let's fly her in a balloon', he offered; at
First Berthe's other children and grandchildren laughed;
Then they decided to give it a shot. 'It'd be great
Fun to watch granny floating in a balloon!' giggles
Michiel's cheeky little Ivy. And Berthe lingering on
Their real intention takes them on, Ludo assuring
Her she'd not fly alone, he'd sit right next to her;
Martin & Connie then invite us to cross The Chennel
And watch Berthe flying the balloon; we all accept.
But it was the greyest April day in Rhoon Village;
The cloud think; it began to drizzle; Michiel felt
A lump. Why does Rotterdam go suddenly foggy?
Perhaps it wasn't a good idea. Shouldn't we have
Gone to church first? Then the Balloonman rings:
It might be too risky to fly, but he'd get back to us
When the fog clears. Michiel's lump is heavier; then
Ludo, Martin and the children put on their anoraks;
We all put on our anoraks; soon we are combing
The garden's rose shrubs, trees and flowers, calling
Out the Easter eggs we are each picking – the Dutch
Easter has truly begun, balloon-flying forgotten.

II

When the cloud clears Balloonman rings again, 'Let's
Give it a try'; Berthe's face beams; we run to waiting
Cars; Michiel looks lumpy; we jump in with him to
Give him a cheer; Martin & Connie trail us, rather

Shaken too. But to fly a balloon from Tilburg Park
Gather those with families flying; together pin down
The basket bottom as the top rest gas-blows into shape;
(On soft, murky grass it won't be easy). Berthe & Ludo
Haven't got all the time to jump into the burning basket!
'Isn't it nice that other families are flying as well?' Michiel
Only grunts. The lift off is rugged at first then sways!
'Oh, watch that swamp now; Lord, those tall trees!'
And Berthe is gone; but return to cars to give chase.
Balloonman who communicates with Balloonwoman
Makes our guide (though Michiel wonders if any
Person really knows where Berthe's balloon intends
To perch); so, we mustn't take long to refuel the cars
(Or stop to pee). Michiel's getting sour about these
Tedious green fields, the dykes and canals Berthe
Is crossing; when the basket appears to want to land
On a colony of ugly trees, Michiel's driving stops!
We resume nervously waving to Berthe flying lower
And lower until the basket swings, swoops, jerk-lands
On Maren–Kessel farm where caged hounds bark: well
Done, welcome, welkom! Balloonman's glad he's landed
This Catholic side of River Maas; the Calvinist side
Wouldn't let him pick up his balloon Sunday last time;
Balloonman displays his Tilburg letters of credence,
Berthe receives her birthday flying certificate, Michiel
Touches Berthe's bruised hand with sparkling smile!

The Acacias Of Gaborone City, Botswana

(For Pearson Luhanga)

When I first saw these acacias of Gaborone
I flinched at their stubborn roots once harshly
Shattered by the cruel bombs of apartheid,

I wondered why their leaves insolently opened
Up when their brute branches and keen thorns
Tore our careless hands as the brown sparrows

Teasingly hopped about the creamy flowers;
I feared how their grey blended with our hazy
Landscapes too and wished their jacarandas were

Likewise fabricated to shield our barrenscapes;
But today, when I watched this capital branching
In all directions and like other world capital cities

Quietly breeding dual carriageways, I sighed
At their latent malignancies as the chirruping
Sparrows succumbed to the countless car alarms

Tweeting from house to hut; even you thought
Of planting more acacia trees around your house –
To scratch some thief to shame! You despaired.

Warm Thoughts For Ken Saro-Wiwa

I was beginning to recover from the gruesome
Gecko which burst on the blanket rags on my
Knees, after severing from the cobweb rafters
Of my Mikuyu Prison recess, when I heard that

The armed vultures had abducted you again –
My heart aches. I remember your gentle embrace
At Potsdam to salute my release from another
Choking cell, you recalled the freezing breath

That writers globally sprayed on our lion's balls
To loosen its flesh-clutching jaws, I bragged about
The fleas, and swarms of bats pouring stinking shit
Into our mouths as we battled the eternal beasts

Of our wakeful slumbers – you laughed. Today,
You must invoke that humour again, my brother,
And as you marvel at the handcuff scars darkly
Glistening, courage! Watch the cracks on your

Prison walls, let them nimbly hold the razors and
Needles of the life we once endured, let the rapture
Of gracious laughter shared, the memory of justice,
Succour you like a prayer, then as those countless

Scorpions, mosquitoes and cockroaches fuss about
Your walls, remember to reach out for that tender
Cloud which forever hovers above your solitary
Sanctum with out wishes to restore, cheer, hope!

Looking For Nyarwanda
Among The Bones Of Butare

Why have I come to watch this carnage of machete
Slashing each other's banana fronds to death in this
Eternal heat? How do I hope to find a lost friend
Among these godless shrines of Rwanda? Isabela,
Those milky teeth you showed me when you said
Farewell at our language seminar exactly eleven
Years today are stained in blood. I feel hollow and
Cheated. I sat under the canopy of your banana
Leaves as the chicks pecked at their morning grain;
You promised to teach me the real KiNyarwanda as
I could not join the others climbing your mountain
Ranges; and as the village children gathered, keen
To share my first lesson, laughing and bemused by
The words I used – why did they sound like theirs,
I jotted down fifty words in KiNyarwanda from my
Corpus of limited ChiYao from home two thousand
Miles away – the children thought I was lying, I spoke
Their tongue, how could we communicate so easily?

I asked about your banana beer, what did you blend
To produce the delicate flavour so congenial, how
Many days did it need to brew, did you sell it from
The tattooed melon-shaped calabashes I bargained
For at the markets we stopped over, driving between
Kigali and Butare, where you also chose two souvenir
Kitenges, black on white and white on red, for my
Wife to wrap-round? Besides, that pristine Marimba
Orchestra which toured all France in summer, you
Boasted, and which we loved so much at Butare – has
All that come to this? Why did you not warn the Hutu
And Tutsi mementoes I arrogantly clutched would
Soon rend each other to death, human flesh floating

In lakes, rivers and streams like dead leaves? Where,
Where are the gentle children who giggled at my first
Syllables of KiNyarwanda, where in this desecrated
Dust of exodus, this stench of human meat, amongst
These arid bones, Nyarwanda, where are you now?

The Child That Now Hurts

(A Poem for Rwanda)

This child that hurts today was hers
Once, sleeping soundly on her back,
Braced by glowing *kitenge* as mother
Worked the ridges of her millet field;

This son that whimpers in his sleep was
The son she pined for once upon years;
When he cried mum breast-nourished
Him under the shade of her succulent

Banana fronds; this boy turned bones
Strapped on mum's emaciated back was
Hers, running up and down the sausage
Trees of her millet field, inventing cars

From contraptions of bicycle spokes and
Coat-hangers, becoming the man who
Would weave the reed and bamboo granary
For her millet harvest. But when the war

Eventually came, the war between mum's
Brothers' houses, the war without a name,
When this alien encounter spilled bloody
Heavy rains, washing away foundations

Of sausage trees, millet fields, the bananas,
Men, women, children, goats and chickens;
When the grass-thatched houses began to
Crumble, swirling, floating away, mother

Had to run for her life, the son on her back,
Unable to reap the millet of her sweat. Now
Having crossed the thorny bushes, craggy
Cliffs, steep hills and valleys in the exodus

Of this hostile amalgam of dust and blood,
This blood whose roots no mum or child
Can fathom, today when his mum's feet
Refuse to lift, badly blistered in her run from

The enemy – her own people; today when
The child on her back gets too ponderous
And the strings of *kitenge* biting severely into
Her shoulder's flesh snap, even the mother

Must retire and lay her son by the way-side
For the foraging hyenas to assault – better
That indignity of ravaging beasts than dying
With his bones forever girlded on her back.

Chitenje For A Lifetime Wedding Cheer

(For George & Becky Harrison, Durham Cathedral, 1996)

And tonight, when the uncles, aunts & elders
Gather beside the nervous light of the flaming
Candles & paraffin lamps; when they spread
Their ancient mat, from timeless baobab tree
Trunks, on your floor & they invite you both
To consummate their exhortatory tales of heroic
Wed-locks of long ago; neither weep at their
Bawdy tales nor waste your lamentation in silent
Capitulation; for you are noble people, neither
Bonded to the elders nor their tales & mind these
Elders, they tend to define things in easy black
& white; you deserve subtler shades of colour;
God has endowed you with rare brown delicately
Drenched in rare pink wedded to precious love;
So, when we offer you this traditional hoe, this
Chitenje, we do not mean you to dig the rolling
Green valleys of Wales or the mystic mountain ranges
Of Malawi; for hoes are signs & *chitenjes* mere
Covers – outward icons. The serious business of
Love & tolerance begins when you smile after
Your first quarrel & eyes sparkle at each parting;
May this hoe then, this *chitenje* & these words
Bring you the wedding cheer of a lifetime, love!

Remembering The Tyrant's
Game Of Football, 1978

Now that our national football team brings
Home the coveted East and Central African
Football Challenge Cup and the announcer's
Husky excitement with the winning goal still
Blasts our wireless, reverberating between
Blantyre and Nairobi, may the dustbin tom-
toms of Ndirande township, the midnight
Buckets of Soche Mountain and the scratchy
Rhythms of tin-cans throughout the territory
Clamour with rapture unknown to applaud
The nation's singular accomplishment; and
Why should the children for once not dance
To their troupe's triumph though to achieve
Is to commit a crime here? Let the band crack
The country's banned casks of mirth – when
This babe let out its first cry, grannies and all
Jumped with joy, breaking its umbilical cord,
But their hurrahs were deflated by the Father
Of the nation-for-life who saw such humour
As rebellion against his might. Yet as the boys
Bring their cup, we'll claim the village dance
Again, prancing about dusty roads, shuffling
Along murky sidewalks festooned in khaki –
dry banana leaves, monkey and fox skin hats
Of long ago; today we'll make our own *nyau*
Dancers again, casting our stilts and hands up,
Down, about, dancing the moonlight dance,
Defying the despotic times; but when the Party
Fetches the desired East and Central African
Trophy, these times of our political quarantine,
Spoof the beast into tapping his eminent-foot-
for-life; and why not, when the football game

He created in his life image to dimwit sharper
Schemes these fifteen years, has got him this
Resounding honour of his life time? So, as our
Lads return tomorrow, ensnare the life-tyrant into
Trebling his prize of the local tournament – we
Vow to keep away from his political football!

The Return Of The Rhinoceros

(Letters home for Anthony Nazombe, Edge Kanyongolo
& those who fought for the new political landscape, 1994)

I

We all feared their return would be a matter of course
Those petrifying rhinoceros of Liwonde Game Park
Now safely tamed among the elephants and hippos
Of home; it's a shame it took so many innocent snouts
And horns, so much bloodshed of brother kill brother
Take task, shame it took so many sweating armpits,
So many bloody festivals, the prayers, warm thoughts
These years, to realise that sooner or later we would
Have to restore this badly jaded Liwonde Game Park –
Giving back the precious rhinoceros' snouts and horns
We foreign-exchanged for swollen Swiss Accounts or
Carelessly flung to the drug arenas of Californian exiles
Where other rhinos are bravely rested. Are these new
South African game rangers the Mandela syndrome we
Once trusted? May their precious gestures multiply.

II

And today I remember those 'Kudya Discovery Lodge'
Hippopotami we loved so much by Liwonde Game Park,
I recall how hard they blew their noses, shooting water
Jets in the air, and cheering our external examining sister
Micere fuming from our airport prudes for shamelessly
Ripping her trousers straight from Oslo instead of simply
Warning, 'Women no trousers, men short hair here!' No
Matter. So, what happened to the other hippos after your
Triumphant referendum? Did they perhaps stomp about
The reed shores of Liwonde Game Park, foaming, undone
When they saw the ancient rhinoceros returning to camp?
What tune did the whimpering Naisi pythons and Kabula
Hill cheetahs sing as you marched the jacaranda avenues

174

Of home? What verse crossed the Likangala and Ndirande
Bridges to cover our rebels from the wrath of the gods?

III

And should I have been there you honestly reckon,
To hobble about, hit the bull's eye, perhaps help with
The Carlsberg rounds, as the rhinos returned to lodge?
In times like these your hedging vociferous chameleons
Are the least you need. But the euphoric Diaspora here
Would've loved to have been, these feverish swallows
Criss-crossing the global seasons for warmth, some even
Threatened to 'direct' your theatre in the round though
Obviously beaten by your heroic feat they chose minor
Roles, to publish this, expose that, as the news of those
Familiar clichés arrived – who dares claim more from
This distance? It was the spark of your initial newsletter,
The subterranean 'open' letters, the crunch of the Bishops
Lenten Letter, mass imprisonments, riots, your indelible
Blood that did the nation proud, please take our 'asante!'

IV

Yet this canoe you've scooped for us with the bitter adze
Of the pen, these rhinoceros you've brought back home,
Guard with envy, nurture this rare babe in the warmth
Of the silk shawl our mothers left behind, for, haven't
We seen the return of European guards after burrowing
In the shadows of their own mirrors, haven't we heard
The sinister laughter of midnight jackals, those hyenas
Hooing, the foxes cracking eerie noises, scornful of novel,
Liberated hands fumbling as they devised new charms
To outdo the magic of old cinders, who can imagine our
Old guards playing it otherwise? They too will attempt
To desperately re-mint new alliances and as the world
Has short memory of our funereal eyes irked by the end-
less wakes our guards have hatched, won't they chime:
'In the name of truces, don't take us to courts?' Watch.

The Fish Eagles Of Cape Maclear, 1994*

I

Today, it's the yellow bulldozers that lumber
Up and down the tortuous mountain footpaths,
Digging deep roots of the rocks and the trees
Which block the way to Cape Maclear; cranes
Caterpillars, D-sevens, the lot, gobble rock and
Dirt blustering their way like tropical storms.
The brutes mean to forge sturdy bridges over
Militant mountain valleys, rivers and hearts
Leaving behind thickets of dust for vehicles,
Bikes, mortals, to saunter about; blades slash
New wounds, old wounds heal in the name of
Progress over-looked and this was rugged
Rebel country once and David Livingstone's
Dreams were mortified by mosquitoes here,
No one dared enter these mountain ranges.
But with tyrant-for-life now definitely sorted
The yellow monsters have been brought in,
So when our jeep wailed in the dust driving
Here this morning and tourist Mozambicans
Bound for the beach were stranded, it's these
Beasts that rescued us. Today, we've deserted
The salty waters of Europe for the lap-lapping
Breakers of the lake, we've come back home
For the curative waters to cleanse the hurt
Of three decades of despotic desires; we've
Come back home to watch fish eagles swoop
Down and nestle on baobab tree branches as
Cape Maclear fishermen haul ashore twine
Laden with prime *kampango* and *chambo*.†

II

So, as the tender breeze blows the evening
Beach to your face, Uncle, pick up the pebbles,
Skim them on the lake's temperate breakers
In memory of your childhood games; take these
Beach children, bare, thrilled by the cameras
Of our London filming crew, only three decades
Into independence this year have they begun
Their schooling without fees; the bold broad
Smiles on their faces declare their thirst for
Learning. And hoping to stir you with the Maths
And English he has learnt today one child,
Having run home, offers his exercise books
For you to check, boasting fourteen, recently
Circumcised (his younger folk mock his age
And clash of customs but his resolve to learn
Is enormous); your eyes glazed by unbridled
Tears manifest the pending paradoxes of our
Predicament; you want to float away, perhaps
To weep but gallantly choose the wet turtle
Canoe from where you decide to minister to
Your beach children; when our vehicle's stuck
In the sand (the mountain fool was tempting
The jeep along the sand!), you marshal your
Beach village to rescue, as I submit to distant
Colonies of huddled rocks, white with seagull
Droppings, where the island's fish eagles sing
Those familiar melodies of long ago. My dear
Uncle, welcome to the beach you spent half
Your life pining for, relish these rungs of drift –
wood as the slugs wash among the knotted blue
Water lilies and the frogs dive underneath, but
As you separate the beach snail shells you once

Gathered for porridge spoons, hear my iniquity:
When I rebelled against whoever in this land
I only thought you'd offer us another poem!

*Composed on taking David Rubadiri, Malawi's most
distinguished poet and educationist to Cape Maclear after
his return to Malawi from 30 years of exile – thanks to the
BBC Television crew who took us there.*

†*Salmon and tilapia*

Guilty Of Nipping Her Pumpkin Leaves, 1994

(For Hangsan-Mpalive Msika)

I

The fear of dying without paying for those
Pumpkin leaves he pinched from her stall
Brings him here, though she fiercely declares
Total innocence of the time and vegetables
She lent him seven years ago; she cannot recall
When the pigeon was 'taken' or the swallow
Wafted to those dissonant frosty habitats to
Gather twigs to nest its young after grudgingly
Revoking the blinding mirages of the sandy
Beaches of the home to which he now returns;
Her vegetable hutch is still organic, though
Grown surer, but she attests vague memory
Of the pigeon and his story – Oh time, how
Could you be so callous as to sever memories
So precious when all he desires is to redress
The anguish of nipping her pumpkin leaves?

II

Her altercation becomes bolder: is he serious,
Could he have returned home to ridicule her
Nudity with his cameras as strange visitors
In the dead monster's regime once did, has he
Got no shame for asserting the resurrection
Of the best customer she once boasted about,
Now presumed dead? No, she would have none
Of his alien stratagems nor would she license
Another of her own grins to enter his cameras,
Tourist or traveller; today the market deals
In graver business, grimaces of her children's
Tatters have fattened the albums of the likes

Of him before, they got the patches for their
Generous gestures instead; she would not offer
Any of her children as prey to another natty
Gimmick, never! 'Not today with the beast
Gone, never if he should decide to resurrect!'

III

'Woman, I hear your passion, I too withheld
The spite I felt for the beast to save my life
And my children but do you not remember
That son-in-law living in Mulungusi Avenue
Whom you buoyantly married your daughters
Every time he visited this stall? Do you not
Remember the groundnuts and spinach you
Lent this face that paid back each month-end?
Well, the turtle has come back home to pay
For the pumpkin leaves and okra he nibbled
From this faltering shack those many years ago;
Here, take your money which has tormented
Me in my prison and exile these many years!'
Even his London filming crew is unmoved by
His confession under the market's jacarandas –
It's not in the script for their tale of his return!

IV

Then rubbing her eyes to weigh the ghost she
Gibes in disbelief, 'They are all returning home
Those buffaloes who left these kraals many dry
Seasons ago; as for you my son, what kept you?
My daughters are too old for you now, why did
You not despatch your uncle or some emissary
For the bride price up front? Today, the price of
The pumpkin leaf you knew has more than trebled;
It continues to climb, though with the lion-for-life
Permanently settled the options in our vegetable
Calling are multiplying; the land is still desert

But whoever dreamt that the fiend would go for
The thundering rains to pour? Imagine no man,
No woman strips us naked for Party Cards at
The market gates any more!' Then grasping his
Hand she shoves his money into her camisole
And gazes right past him to the next customer!

Hyenas Playing Political Prisoners

(For Fred, James, Marshal & Cuthbert)

'The hyenas are playing political prisoners
Now, wishing your exile well and regretting
They were not imprisoned by the monster,
Things would have been fine for them too!'

But brethren, who stopped you, who's it that
Said, 'To kill a baboon do not look into his
Face, lest you bear remorse', who's it that
Shouted, 'Enjoy while it lasts!', and anyway,

Why did you pervert the recent opportunity,
Where were you when your toilet cleaners,
Your students, secretaries, messengers, drivers,
Market vendors, those urban and rural criers

(Who really felt the blisters from the chains,
Ropes and knobkerries of our monster-for-life,
From his village and town youths and pioneers
More than you and me those years ago!); where

Was this venom now unleashed, when others
Fearlessly chanted for this new dawn, marching
Along the jacaranda avenues with new banners;
Why did you merely watch, stroking your dry

Chin or twisting your goatee, believing nothing
Would happen as nothing had happened before,
When everyone knew it was you who never let
Anything happen? Shame on you; pity no one

Will dare to take you to the detention camps as
You'd wish, however cacophonous with explicit
Slur your voice maybe today; yet knowing your
Frailty and the pest-riddled red-kidney beans in

Prison, I wonder if you in particular, would not
Have needed more than the ancestral tattoos
On your bottom to come back alive! Perhaps
You should have invented more brazen lore

For the monster-for-life who you informed
About us; but I have a more modest overture:
Now that no one will harass you given those
New courts around you, today that you are

Back, carousing better than in your despotic
Times, why don't you do the honourable thing,
Why not embrace this truer liberation others
Have won for you? And in case you think exile

Is all colour TV and fun, let in another shadow
Tomorrow, you will see what shaved your
Guinea fowl bald, you'll feel the rabid hyenas
Of the political prisoners you seek to play!

The Lies We Told About The Elephant

So, when you turn over the new leaf of
This gentle nation, do not tell the children
Another lie; how wise elephant returned
To his kraal at his own fancy after years
Wandering in alien lands; how elephant
Found fellow elephants naked, starving,
Living in huts that leaked; how grateful
Elephant's folks were when he removed
Their sackcloths, showing them how best
To grow their food on farms; do not lie that
Elephants can be Messiahs that live forever;
For today, the children have watched how
Elephant stuffed himself with vegetable,
Animal, tobacco farms he fabricated all over
Their father's land to his tuneful wealth
Which the hyenas, the cats and others will
Jostle over, after his long-anticipated repose;
The children have seen the palaces that do
Not leak elephant built himself; they can
Feel the nation's pulse elephant left cold.
Besides, as you restore the nation's heroes
And heroines to their glory, devote honest
Footnotes to the foreign ants in elephant's
Flaming years who, fatigued by the infinite
Griefs the elephant forced on his own folks,
Scratched his deaf lobules with their lap-tops,
Faxes, diplomatic bags, their voices and all;
Do not dare another fib, for many invisible
Voices have invested in this victory of ours,
Many more than you will ever conceive!

The New Rebels At Zalewa Highway Bridge

A contraption of split bamboo and crumpled
Empty oil drums has whittled Zalewa Highway
Bridge to single file where all vehicles must stop
For traffic officers to check the bags for guns;

But as the check point boss flicks through my
Wad of T-shirts, a soldier rushes in, swinging
AK47, bringing an urgent message for his boss,
"Sorry, Bwana, but that truck has bandits with

Two AK47s, one's loaded, come rescue, quick';
The boss grins at our coach to proceed running
To the graver task to hand; I refuse to believe
What I hear as uneasy passengers loudly settle

Down to ponder the alien horrors of the times.
Four years ago, this check-point bustled with
Henchpeople who discharged their duties more
Ferociously, hunting the rebels they had largely

Invented to dazzle our lion-for-life; everybody was
Here: army generals, police constables, the dreaded
Young Pioneers, each boasting their own intelligence
As Romania-trained hit squads combed the bushes

Ready to pounce at the slighted stir of rebellion;
Today, this check-point is peopled by characters
Who go about their business with chatter; Young
Pioneers no longer constitute the checking junta,

'Some Young Pioneers crossed into Mozambique
On *Operation Bwezani,* after the life beast's shock
On the political arena!', passengers shout, 'It begun
Like a joke, in Mzuzu city bar, four hundred miles

North, when pioneers challenged soldiers to duel
And unable to subdue the soldiers, one pioneer
Ran home, brought a pistol, shot several soldiers
Dead; whereupon the whole battalion mounted

Operation Bwezani, crushing all paramilitary
Pioneer bases throughout the land, confiscating
Their armoury, bringing about this delightful new
State! It's the pioneers who cross the borders

That trickle back plundering villages, townships
And cities; it's pioneers, the new rebels, for whom
These check-points are raised, though God knows
Who later booted the liberators out of barracks!'

Behind me the dry mountain ranges, brown valleys
With green splashes of palm and baobab trees reel
Past, as I recollect the potholes to my sister's house
And stroke my chin at the ironies of another time!

When The Watery Monsters Argued

(For Berlings Kaunda)

When he revisited the Milimbo Lagoon of
His childhood, he found it had rock-dried:
His dugout canoe, the driftwood, fish-traps,
The fishing tackle and the worms for bait,
Even the stubborn mudfish had moved on;

Only ghosts, water beasts, surged forward
From the reed bushes of their barren lagoon,
Extending their wise handshakes and arguing,
'Man, neither cast this change of fortunes to
The wind nor reject your ancestral wisdom;

'Do not waste your bitter herb on our bones,
We were mere messengers of your destiny;
Forget the past, forget whatever we inflicted
On you, people are now riding on the dreams
We denied them decades ago; now more than

Ever before this young nation should not be
Allowed to wallow in the past; the exigencies
Of building this glowing nation must precede
Everything and think positive; think future
Without retribution, without malice …' Yet

As the watery presences paddled their fast
Sinking raft to their fish-eagle island invoking
Todays without their yesterdays, he wept at
The blisters of their future without its present,
He began to see what the fiends really meant:

He knew the silence their beastly transition
Offered was neither victory nor antidote for
The wounds the watery freaks had inflicted;
He knew that weathering their weeping scars
Would incite other bitter tears, he then swore,

'Brethren, golden glories are hard to police,
But do not ask us to forget the past, and how
Could poetry forget the past when Africa still
Bleeds from forgetting its past; empower others
To forget your past – my struggle continues!'

New Poems

The Stench Of Porridge

(for Jeoff Thindwa)

Why does the stench of porridge
With maggots and weevils floating,
The scorching heat trapped
Within reeking walls,
The irritation of shrilling
Cicadas and centipedes at night,
The hyenas forever *hooing*,
The scorpion's ugly sting
Splitting down the spine,
Track us wherever we hide?
Why does the daily bending
At strip searches as prison
Guards hunt the anus for
Bogus designs of our escapes,
The monthly purging with
Malaria, cholera, diarrhoea,
The poison pigeon peas,
The Sick Bay queues of skeletal
Limbs craving for valium
To heal deadly silences –
Why does the stench of prison
Suddenly catch us like lust?
Didn't the spirit govern once for all,
The groans of prisoners dying next cell
The pangs of prisoners gone mad,
The weeping blisters on our elbows,
Knees, balls, bums, buttocks, wherever
And the blizzards blustering
The rusty tin roofs
Where helpless chickens
Drip in the storm?

For how long does this
Stench intend to trail us?
Or is it really true what they say,
'Once prisoner always prisoner' –
Why?

It's The Speed That Matters, My Dear Padre

(For Fr Pat O'Malley, Fr Leo Morahan & Landeg White)

It's the speed, my dear padre, the speed with
Which you risk to save one's life that counts.

The chameleon hesitates, often three times,
Before putting his foot down, the squirrel

Lashes its bushy tail before it leaps onto its
Safer baobab branch, the spotted cheetah

Stalks the undergrowth, smarting for her
Final pounce, but nothing happens without

The speed with which they do their deed
My dear padre, the speed is all – for it was

The speed with which you chose to telephone
Speaking in Gaelic, so our tyrant's surrogates

Could not decipher your word – that you had
Seen this bumblebee chained behind their

Security van; it's the speed your Galway Parish
Friend sent the word to our friend in York

To shout to the world for another who'd been
Taken; it's the speed the radio waves recycled

The word across the globe the following day,
Shaming our Life Excellency and his minions,

Shattering their designs to kill; it's the speed
That saved the bumblebee. Even when you

Chose to bury the rebel's mother, regardless,
Alone, dear padre, after University Registrar had

Dared any colleague to bury the rebel's mother,
It was the speed with which you slighted their

Pitiful fears, to minister to the dead as you must;
It's the speed to rescue that matters, dear padre.

On David Constantine's Poem

(for Landeg White & David Constantine)

Your poem for Irina Ratushinskaya
On your birthday has reached these
Putrid African prison walls it
Was probably not meant for;
What cheer distant voices must bring
Another poet crackling in the Russian
Winters of icicle cells, I imagine.
Yet even in this dungeon where
Day after day we fester within
The walls of the tropical summers
Of our life president
And his hangers-on, even here,
What fresh blood flushes
When an unexpected poem arrives,
What fire, what energy
Inflames these fragile bones!
Indeed we have the verses in common,
Notwithstanding
The detention camps
The laws against poems
The black or white
Traitor or patriot
Binary oppositions;
But secure in your
Voices of solidarity,
We'll crush the crocodiles
That crack our brittle bones.
Do not falter then, brother,
Do not waver, dear brethren,
But craft on the verses
Whose ceaseless whisper resonates
Beyond the Whitehalls of our dreams!

On Driving His Political Enemies To Scarborough

(For Kanyama Chiume, David Rubadiri & Felix Mnthali)

And if you should wish me another prison let it be
For rallying within the city of York those rebels you

Could not stomach only weeks of our independence,
Seeking not their scholarly papers, but their learned

Memories of your wrath at the first cabinet and other
Crises you'll doubtless bequeath this tender nation.

And what a conference, what revelations, what cheer!
Did you really get struck off the medical register for

Consuming another man's assets, your own receptionist
Nurse, what is it about receptionist nurses with you? And

Those abortions in Ghana, did you thank the rhinoceros
Who summoned you to liberate your homeland instead?

What treason did you see in the moustache of your
Political enemy number one? What revolt in the verse

Of your UN envoy that we read hidden in our youthful
Blankets and how dare you jail my teacher for being

Just another clever northerner? If you should invent
Another prison for me, let it be for driving your three

Political enemies to Scarborough one English summer
Afternoon, letting them relax to watch Scarborough

196

Children surfing with the seagulls and riding the tender
Crests and splashes of the calm bay; let it be for buying

Your rebels huge portions of Scarborough fish'n'chips,
Sitting at the wooden table to analyse the songs your

Dancing witches sang to you; let it be for good reason
Not the conjectures of your mistress about my treason!

Rested Amongst Fellow Hyenas, Finally

(for David Kerr)

So the undertakers have buried
Their lion of the nation for life
Among the hyenas he ridiculed
At political rallies once? Have

They embalmed their notable
In his waistcoat, striped dark
Suit, bowler hat, overcoat and
The sunglasses that screened

Their endless anxieties too? Did
The woodpeckers, squirrels, cats
And snakes spit in disbelief as
The fly whisk which swiped their

Laughter shut was placed on
His right – lest another mosquito
Zang past to upset his eternal
Glory? And did the gravediggers

Afterwards truly return to harvest
His flaming garlands for their
Next highest bidding client, one
By one, dancing their dance of

Witches as the palm leaf flames
Flattered in the dark? Did they
Ask about the lavish banquets,
The farms his hangers-on will

Scramble over? What welcome did
His Young Pioneer invented rebels
Give him on arrival? Did they ask
How it felt to be finally there, alone?

And were those battles he fought
To become another Almighty God
Worth spilling his people's blood
For, eventually? And will the taxis

Really show us the solitary barbed
Wire cemetery where his rabid hyenas
Gather at night stomping about and
Foaming for his bones – glory be!

The Minster Inn, York

When Robinson Crusoe grabbed his fishing rod
Hopped onto the driftwood constricted to the grass

Thicket of the lagoon and floated away, singing
About the gods of tilapia and mudfish which had

Steered his life hitherto, did he expect to land
Among the aliens he'd long feared for rejecting

The cloud upon which other fairies were meant to
Flutter? But when he saw the goblins gasping for

Fresh air in their drunken cellars, too ashamed
To invoke the gods they'd long shunned, Crusoe

Bloated his familial proverb: when handshakes go
Beyond the elbow, brother, move on, before their

Battles begin; yet pondering the worms for bait
Strewn among the childhood fish traps of home

And watching the imminent 'glories' of their New
Millennium, Crusoe began to dither and, choosing

The corner pedestal of the city's Public House, he
Too carelessly burped, 'I'm only here for the beer!'

Fleeting Child Of The 3-Day Week

Hang on, Mister, I too was here when
The Winter of Discontent broke out
And London bin men let London stink.

I was here when 3-day week closed our
Libraries at 5.30 each day and my friend
And I rushed for Goodge Street Tube

Station, headed for the Circle Line that
Twirled us round, round, round, round –
'Studying in the round' we christened

It – until 'All Change' brought us back
To Lillian Penson Hall to watch Trevor
McDonald's ITV news at 10. When those

In high places insisted on their lives being
Covered but let Green Goddesses lumber
Awkwardly up people's streets to quench

Their fires, refusing to see their poodles'
Muck on the asphalt, I noted the jokes.
Our Commonwealth numbers in Sussex

Gardens voted in Paddington's Labour
MP too! And when the Brixton-Wood
Green riots blazed, they stopped my car

At Tally Ho to hear if I spoke Birmingham
– Where they thought the riots originated.
Besides, you've never watched Notting

Hill Carnival from Chepstow Road nor
Published poems in Alan Ross's *London
Magazine* – with real poets! Where were

You when they knocked out Red Ken for
The socialist GLC they invented? What have
You done to dub me economic migrant?

What do you know about the economics
Migrants suffer? By your piddling dossier
You have not even run from IRA Tube

Station bomb scares! Get real then, if you
Are truly serious about your global village,
This is no fleeting child of your 3-day week!

After Celebrating Our Asylum Stories At West Yorkshire Playhouse, Leeds

So, define her separately,
She's not just another
Castaway washed up your
Rough seas like driftwood,
It's the nameless battles
Your sages burdened her
People that broke her back;
Define him differently,
He's not another squirrel
Ousted from your poplars,
It's the endless cyclones,
Earthquakes, volcanoes,
Floods, mud and dust that
Drafted him here; define
Them warmly, how could
Your economic émigré queue
At your job centres day after
Day? If you must, define us
Gently, how do you hope
To see the tales we bear
When you refuse to hear
The whispers we share?

The Seashells Of Bridlington North Beach

(for Mercy Angela)

She hated anything caged, fish particularly,
Fish caged in glass boxes, ponds, whatever;

'Reminds me of prisons and slavery,' she said;
So, when first she caught the vast green view

Of Bridlington North Beach shimmering that
English summer day, she greeted the sight like

A Sahara girl on parched feet, cupping, cupping,
Cupping the water madly, laundering her palms,

Giggling and laughing. Then rubbing the hands
On her skirt, she threw her bottom on the sandy

Beach and let the sea breathe in and out on her
As she relaxed her crossed legs – 'Free at last!'

She announced to the beach crowds oblivious;
And as the seascape rallied and vanished at her

Feet, she mapped her world, 'The Netherlands
We visited must be here; Norway, Sweden there;

Beyond that Russia!' Then gathering more sea-
shells and selecting them one by one, she turned

To him, 'Do you remember eating porridge from
Beach shells once?' He nodded, smiling at another

Memory of the African lakes they were forced to
Abandon. 'Someday, perhaps I'll take that home

To celebrate!' She said staring into the deep sea.
Today, her egg-like pebbles, her pearls of seashells

Still sparkle at the windowsill; her wishes still ring,
'Change regularly the water in the receptacles to

Keep the pebbles and seashells shining – you'll
See, it's a lot healthier than feeding caged fish!'

No Swearing, Please, We've Children About

Should you, therefore, perhaps feel a little incarcerated,
Should GNER carriages start jerking, squeaking, shrieking

To a halt, then picking up speed for the umpteenth time;
Should the impassive passengers in time begin to twitch

At the official voices piping through, lavishly apologising
About the delay, do not despair; imagine the explosion

That might have been near the Gas Station, if the fire
Had flared beyond repair as you screeched from your

Reading at Stirling. And forget the fellow fidgeting with
His crossword beside you, forget the lass babbling over

Her mobile phone – still chilling out on her party last night!
When GNER finally squeals at 'Darlington Station Stop'

Another train will be waiting, as sterner reminders bellow
About taking your baggage before you transfer to platform 4

But watch, watch when the reality eventually strikes home,
Watch the passengers suddenly ablaze and damning this,

Damning that, rubbishing this, rubbishing GNER's selfish
Directors, invoking the 'f' words you never thought their

Crosswords would imbibe; and when you 'settle' in your
New seat, do not let the lady beside you hot up about her

Booking arrangements disrupted, lest you miss the bigger
Picture: 'No swearing, please, we have children about!'

When Chameleon First Saw
The City Of Cork

(For Colbert Kearney, 1999)

When chameleon first saw
The city of Cork
Huddled among her seven hills,
The coves cannily caved in
By the two bows of River Lee,
He wondered how
She survived without her cellars;
Then there was that
Ubiquitous Irish anger:
Christ this Christ that,
Fuck this fuck that,
Shit this shit that
Shit every flaming where!
And the puffing
In the public houses
The pipes puffing
The cigars puffing
The joints puffing
Puffing here
Puffing there
Puffing every smoking where!
But when chameleon
Limped beyond the public houses,
Kicking the brick wall here
The scaffoldings there,
Hobbling up the steep cobbles
Of St Patrick's Hill Road –
To hear the glowing
Church spires pleading
To God Almighty;

When he dared
The city's feeble feet
As they shuffled to mass
At the Franciscans
In the nippy Easter mist,
When even chameleon joined
Their 'Easter 16 Parade'
On Western Road
   −   A more serious affair than
      Notting Hill Carnival or
      The mask dances of home
He began to hear
The Corkonian anger
Embedded apparently in 'Ireland' itself
And why Corkonian
Sentences ended on
High tones like the Geordies'
Of North East England.
But, of course, Cork's
European façade of
Fuck this fuck that
Puff here puff there
Fucking and puffing
Every bleeding where
Only arrived when Cork's
Perhaps finest poet
In Irish insisted on
Stilling his nerves
On Cork's own
Jameson 12
Neat from its
Rude glasses!

The Grumpy Old Hippopotami Of Tala
Game Reserve, KwaZulu Natal, 1999

(For Matthew Sweeney)

Tell them to emulate the ostriches who accost their
Snoops by attenuating their necks, walking tall on

The brown sedges, grasses and ferns of their Tala Game
Reserve; tell them to watch the giraffes who peak

Their ears above the acacia treetops then, unruffled
By their own majesty, slouch their welcome, nibbling

At the little green leaves between the sharp thorns.
Why don't they delight like the secretary birds who,

After stroking each other, their ponytails flaunting
In the winter breeze, draw out their wings, fly-dancing

And mock-fighting their aerial display before us; why
Don't they marvel at the black rhinoceri that block our

Tracks, refusing to begrudge us the spectacle of their mum's
Protracted piercing piss? Tell them even hippopotami

Can master the craft of the resplendent wildebeest,
The nimble antelope and agile zebra; and insist they are

Mere hippopotami blown into the lake by the burden
Of chance, if they want to get on here, they will have

To fluster at whatever gull picks their noses next time,
They'll have to grunt at the interlopers who want progress

On their estate – if it's apartheid they still bemoan, tell
Them, 'Forget it, the brute will never come back!'

The Patron Of Jubilee 2000

(Celebrating the Life of Mwalimu Julius Nyerere
of Tanzania, 19 April 2000, London)

I should have engaged your mind
In your modest village house where
The Kilimanjaro beacon shone through

The political fevers of the Great Rift
Valley; not in my undergraduate
Essays on dead empires and stubborn

Despots, along dusty nondescript
Corridors of campuses beside another
Independence Arch of minor rift

Valleys; for, when the leopard leapt
I beheld the foreign foxes panic at
The contested ground; I spied Black

Ant creep up elephant's ears and sting,
Sting, sting until the beast of apartheid
Dropped dead. Our very flamingos

Peeped through the spy-holes of their
Prisons as your People's Women's League
Pleaded with their despot's official Mama

To get her to break the chains around
Our fragile bones. And what images,
What rhythmic tapestry, what symbols

Haunt your Swahili *Julius Caesar* and
The Merchant of Venice! No wonder
This gazelle still enthuses over your

Ujamaa this *ujamaa* that mostly *ujamaa*
About the liberation of the entire Great Rift
Valley. But gazing from your haven now,

Does Black Ant blush as grasshoppers
Fumble over present global injustices?
No matter, patron of peace, *harambee*!

Now That Sept. 11 Should Define
Mr Western Civilisation …

(For Sarah Maguire & Saadi Yousef)

I remember being summoned to the British Council Office
Once, back home; I'd got the Commonwealth Scholarship

Bound for the University of London. The British Council
Lady who interviewed us declared, to get the full benefit

Of our studies in metropolitan Britain, we were to listen
Carefully to what she had to say about 'civilisation' – she

Uttered the word as if it were some Country Squire we
Should've been told about at our village school long ago

Or perhaps some gentleman once in a striped suit, bow
Tie, bowler hat, about to sit at table glittering with silver

Cutlery, ready to eat the precious bits and bobs we'd
Never hope to taste. For the lady first fell into a deadly

Trance and, as if in defence of the law she feared we'd
Soon break, stressed, 'If you do not listen, you'll be

Embarrassed when you are invited to civilised homes!'
Meaning where people ate with knives, folks, spoons;

Drank from mugs, cups, glasses; not with hands, sticks
And shards like us, drinking from calabashes or gourds!

The lady then showed us how the civilised table was
To be set, with the number of plates minutely spaced

Before us, the knives on the right, the folks on the left,
Knives and spoons on top; which knives went with

Which folks with which food; how we were to begin
With the knives and folks outside the plates and moved

Inside, as it were. 'Quaffing one's drink like American
Cowboys won't do!' She insisted, 'You know what I

Mean!' Of course, we did not know what she meant
Until after entering the British Council Head Office at

65 Davis Street, London, SW1, where the lady's rules
Of engagement drastically changed. Now, weren't we

Urged to, 'Join those Bond Street corner shop queues for
Lunch!' And there, didn't we have to pick our fish'n'chips

With our flipping fingers, from the cones of London's
Evening Standard Newspaper? Walking down Portobello

Market that evening, didn't we laugh, laugh, laugh until
We broke wind, tears running down cheeks, imagining

The British Council lady's rules so carelessly breached by
Her own mates! That was years ago, though now that 9/11

Defines Lord Western Civilisation of the New Millennium
I thought you might like to hear when first I met the guy!

Letter To Landeg White In Portugal, Oct. 2001

The sycamores and poplars you abandoned
have begun to cast their brown along the cold
pavements; soon the soggy leaves will bring

the electric trains to their knees, shaming our
advanced civilisation and the charcoal grey
avenues will shudder under the dull English

winter. Yorkshire supermarkets are already
haggling over prices of computer gimmicks
for the children at Halloween, Guy Fawkes

and Christmas; another Mama and Papa on TV
will doubtless stammer over the cheap crackers
that blew up their child's fingers – threatening

the foreign dealers with the summons. Indeed
the New Millennium has been and gone, who-
ever said eat and drink, the end's neigh, will

have to read the signs of the times again. But
how's it with you there, won't the sardines too
reduce to the famous 9/11 binary opposition?

Driving along the narrow lanes of Yorkshire
dales today, alone, I remembered the pheasants
we hunted in your rusty Nissan, weaving down

God's colourful canvas spanning the land –
stuff TESCO's frozen stuffing, let's hunt
fresh birds to celebrate our liberation from

The African crocodiles, we thought, but not
a pheasant's wretched feather crossed our
lanes then nor today! My dear friend, don't

you sometimes wonder at the wisdom of these
places we are forever trading – you among smoking
Portuguese grapes gathering another nest, yours

truly still spelling his name amidst these mouldy
hedgerows? When will our fabulous rodent show
up – if only to tone up God Almighty's dales!

The Taxis Of North Yorkshire

It's how you trusted them so easily
With the story of your life that puzzled,
The way you rushed for the front seat,
Quickly belted up, perhaps apologised
For the slight delay or the Vale of York
Drizzle you brought onto their seats
Before you bombarded them with tales
Of the world you never really shared.
'How dare she walk out on me after
These years?' you began, and chattered
On about the kids, the mortgage, the car
And what to do when she's finally gone.
Often it was the taxis themselves who
Instigated it – 'We are back then, how
Was it where we've been this time?'
And you began your liberal lecture on
Whatever they neither wanted to hear
Nor cared about. Their reaction to their
Radio's social critique was provocative:
'That'll be our learned journalists, at it
Again, the usual crap, if you ask me!'
And titillated you added, 'Don't they
Really believe in the glorious *general public*
They invent and so eloquently speak for!'
About the local elections they knew who
Was coming in and who going out often
Musing, 'What's wrong with politicians,
Why can't they see what we the ordinary
Folk see?' And you rattled your 'whys'
Forever and ever. They had encyclopaedic
Knowledge of the scoops at the horse races
And football pools; boasted about the rich
And the famous they'd driven, the football

Hooligans who had high-jacked their
Taxis at weekend binges – 'Oh, how
Those Saturday gate crashers got sick!'
They warned about the cities' dodgy pubs
And alleyways too; but the taxis you so
Dearly loved were at their brightest when
They brandished what they thought you
Needed to think before you offered them
The tip and rolled your baggage home.

The Ballad Of Lady Bibby Renaissance Of Barrow Docks, April 2003

When Lady Bibby Renaissance first
Docked at the gateway to the Lake
District, seven years ago, her arrival
Was hailed with bagpipe and string;

She would charm the lakes and waters
With her glittering jewels and pearls
People said; she'd particularly make
A fine five star hotel drifting on her

200 luxury beds, thought one business
Tycoon – a frill casino on the Irish Sea
That would surpass Las Vegas casinos
More like, challenged another; please

Deck her in rebel colours, give us another
Radio Caroline on The Irish Sea, cried
Mr Dee Jay – indeed Lady Bibby was
Everyone's premadona until the Home

Secretary offered to crown her Britain's
Cutting Edge "Floating Prison" which'd
Sail in and out of the Irish Channel, free.
When placards against the plan arrived

However, the idea of Lady B was shelved,
Until now when the War in Iraq has begun
And threatens to last beyond its remit.
So, we thought we'd bring Abbotsmead

School children to see if Lady Bibby could
Mount weapons of mass destruction for
Iraq; but alas, we found her in tattoos,
Rusty tears dripping down her cheeks,

Chains that anchored her to dock, rotting.
'But I am just an abject shell, children!' She
Sobbed, defying the billets that valued her
3-story edifice. Neither her blistering ribs

Nor the ripples painfully smiling at her
Remembered whether Lady B of Barrow
Docks had come from The Netherlands,
Switzerland or Sweden and why she chose

To idle at the gateway to the Lake District
– Basking beside the *Pacific Crane* which
Commandeers plutonium and other grave
Nuclear wastes to Japan and back. Perhaps

Abbotsmead school children were right –
When the War in Iraq is over, Lady B will
Feel the blows we dealt her and crumble –
In protest againt the lies we told about her!

Justine Cops Of Clapham Village

When you flagged me down
After the roundabout that says
To Kendal 45 miles, I stopped,
In spite of the warnings never
To, however burdened the hikers
Seemed; I guess it was the blinking
Tractors on A59 refusing to give
Way to the madness of my driving
Week after tedious week, from
The vale of York to the minnows
Of Grasmere – to eke out another
Raw exile – I guess it was the fatigue
That did it, when at times, even
The most careful driver felt doped
By the stink of manures fabricated
Within those timeless hedgerows:
Pig shit here, cow-dung there, and
The sheep everywhere flung like
Khaki turtles in African kraals –
Indeed there were times when
The steering wheel slipped as if
Touched by vandaline anti-climb
And I suffered to share the spirited
Smells of the lovely dales with
Another, living from pillar to post.

It was after the coppers suddenly
Showed up in my mirror as you
Struggled to belt up, shivering from
The hangovers of your whisky and
Soda binges of yester weeks, you
Said, that the insufferable whiff
Of joint from your scruffy anorak

Began to bother – were the coppers
Really following you or was that
Your roundabout trap of getting
Me nicked for picking up the joint-
smoking hiker? So, when you chose
The front seat, Justine Cops, when
You wondered why the sojourner
You called Black Samaritan was
Deaf to your compliments after
God's people had ignored your
Pleading thumb – it's the coppers
I was nervous about. Was I relieved,
Therefore, when you yelled, 'Here,
This junction is home, Clapham
Village!' as the coppers drove past,
Happily, and I recalled another
Clapham Junction I once knew.

Jack Mapanje, Malawi's best known poet, linguist, editor and human rights activist, was born of Yao and Nyanja parents in Mangochi district, southern Malawi. He went to Kadango Anglican School, Chikwawa Catholic Mission School and Zomba Catholic Secondary School. He has a BA degree majoring in English and a Diploma in Education from the University of Malawi. He joined the staff of the English Department, Chancellor College, University of Malawi in 1972, went to the University of London Institute of Education to read for an MPhil degree in English and Education (1975) and University College London where he read for a PhD degree in Linguistics.

In 1984 he became head of English Department at Chancellor College and chairperson of the Linguistics Association SADC universities (LASU), serving nine universities of Africa south the Sahara, which he helped to found in 1984. In June 1985 *Of Chameleons and Gods* was withdrawn from school, college, university, and national libraries and bookshops throughout the country by a directive from Hastings Banda's censorship board. In 1987 he was imprisoned at the notorious Mikuyu Prison in Zomba, without trial and without charge. After nearly four years of incarceration Mapanje was released principally because of international protests from writers, linguists and human rights activists throughout the world.

Mapanje has travelled extensively as a poet, linguist, external examiner and a human rights activist. He has had three books of poetry published: *Of Chameleons and Gods* (Heinemann, Oxford, 1981), *The Chattering Wagtails of Mikuyu Prison* (Heinemann, Oxford, 1993) and *Skipping Without Ropes* (Bloodaxe Books, 1998). He has co-edited *Oral Poetry From Africa: an anthology* (Longmans, 1983), *Summer Fires: New Poetry of Africa* (Heinemann, Oxford, 1983) and *The African Writers' Handbook* (African Book Collective, Oxford, 1999). He recently edited the highly acclaimed African prison anthology, *Gathering Seaweed: African prison writing* (Heinemann, Oxford, 2002).

Jack Mapanje, one of the original members of the writers' group in Malawi, is a recipient of the Rotterdam International Poetry Award (1988) for Of Chameleons and Gods. He was also awarded the USA's Fonlon-Nichols Award (2002) and an honorary doctorate from the University of Stirling, Scotland, for his contribution to poetry and human rights. He has held academic scholarships at the University of York and Oxford University and writers' residences at the University of Leiden, The Netherlands, The Open University, Milton Keynes and University College Cork, the Republic of Ireland. For three years he taught African and Caribbean Literature, Literature of Incarceration and Creative Writing in the School of English, University of Leeds. He has run creative writing workshops in schools, colleges, community centres, city libraries as well as prisons throughout the UK. He worked for three years as the Royal Literary Fund Fellow based at Trinity and All Saints College, University of Leeds. For the past two years he has been poet-in-residence at the Wordsworth Trust, Dove Cottage, Cumbria, where he has been writing his prison memoir. He is now teaching in the School of English at the University of Newcastle upon Tyne. Mapanje lives in the city of York with his family.